Praise for

T0032730

Return on Hum......y

As we hurtle towards a future dominated by data, algorithms and AI, a book about the importance of humanity is perfectly timed and a must-read.

—*Sir John Hegarty, Co-founder and Creative Director at The Garage Soho & The Business of Creativity*

This book has restored my faith in humanity, thank you! It is very easy to get caught up in a corporate world and forget that we have control over the way we behave with each other, the way we interact with the world around us, and we can't operate in a vacuum. The stories of resilience, flexibility, collaboration and cooperation bring to life the fact that truly knowing who you are and how you behave allows each and every one of us to purposefully make our world, including our working world, better.

—*Sam Theobald, Chief People Officer, Next15*

In today's transparent world, power is finally shifting back to its rightful owners – customers and employees. In this world, there will be nowhere for companies to hide. Behaviour will be everything. *Return on Humanity* gives us all a reason to be optimistic and to believe that capitalism – done the right way – is a force for good.

—*Simon Rogerson, Chief Executive Officer, Octopus Group*

A mind-expanding collection of insights, reality checks and actions for a global culture desperately needing to shift our way of being. Transforming from entity-as-machine to entity-as-living-system guided by *Return on Humanity*, clarity of intention can create changes today to create a better tomorrow.

—*Michael Jager, Co-founder and Creative Director, Solidarity of Unbridled Labour*

Managers talk strategy – Leaders tell stories. Philippa has gathered a magnificent set of stories that are sometimes charming, brutally honest and inspiring. She has a compelling way of cutting to the chase, while taking the time to paint a colourful picture of just how every business leader can make a telling difference. You won't find any of this on an MBA course, as this is authentic, vulnerable, and at times, painful. You will be continually inspired to get up, speak up and make a difference. The timing could not be better, and everyone needs a compelling story that enables them to picture themselves making a difference – we salute you!

—René Carayol MBE, World Leading Executive Coach

This is a book which simply radiates hope, optimism and goodness of heart. Although the topic is leadership, this is more than a leadership manual: it's a compendium of wisdom about how to deal more sensitively, humanely and effectively with people and institutions. If only this could be compulsory reading for everyone in power. *Return on Humanity* deserves to achieve recognition and readership, influencing our collective understanding of what makes true leadership and becoming part of the standard by which leaders are judged in the future. I urge you to read it and spread the word.

—Simon Anholt, Founder, Good Country Index

Reading this book is like talking to a very smart friend: it's so easy to read, full of memorable anecdotes and practical tips, and simply very inspiring. I love the way it reframes diversity of talent and thinking, and makes it feel achievable. As a brand strategist, I will be able to use the stories and data in this book to encourage my clients to embrace a more human and diversity-focused approach to leadership, in the knowledge they will come out better for it. This book should be on every business leader's 2024 'to read' list.

—Senta Slingerland, Co-founder of Fala and Founder of 'See It Be It'

This is a fascinating and wonderful book. Its theme is the overlooked and neglected importance of feelings in the commercial world. Philippa uses beautiful stories from around the world to illustrate how we can transform our approach to business. It's also a timely reminder of our responsibilities as human beings. *Return on Humanity* will help you become a real human and a better leader (in that order).

—Harry MacAuslan

This profound contribution to leadership in the modern business world had me at the title. Its welcome succinctness belies its breadth, and it provides refreshing new perspectives on what leadership means and needs to mean in a post shareholder value-centric world. *Return on Humanity* is full of accessible strategies and suggestions as to how to inject more humanity into business and leadership. Who would have thought that humanity might have such a role to play in human enterprise?

—*Matt Symonds, Partner, Altair*

In the context of global instability and the growth of AI, how timely is a book focused on the importance of being human to the world of business: a sense of belonging, the importance of connection, living outside your comfort zone. Philippa's book is a reminder that companies aren't machines, they are simply communities of people. She has lived the past 20 years of her life taking a theory and putting it into practice and has filled her book with simple and yet powerful stories. Step outside of your own world and get into this one.

—*Elliot Moss, Partner and Chief Brand Officer,*
Mishcon de Reya LLP

By shedding a light on seemingly ordinary life moments, Philippa reminds us that the human traits that make us better leaders are found in the very nature of humans and in our everyday interactions. Through life stories from all corners of the world, Philippa shows us that our humanity is the most extraordinary force we have to unlock the only type of leadership that can transcend the volatility of the world we live in today. A must-read for everyone, not just leaders, in a time when we all desperately need to be reminded of the humanity that unites us all.

—*Juliana Xavier, Brand Strategist and Head of Brand*
Management at Yara International

An inspiring and enjoyable read. Packed with stories and wisdom that illuminates the vital importance of humanity in business, guides us to the solutions and reminds us that change is possible, and we are all part of it.

—*John Rosling, Chief Executive Officer, Contexis*

Steven Spielberg once said that he makes movies for the masses but talks to them one at a time. I suspect that readers will engage with *Return on Humanity* in exactly the same way. With examples ranging from marketing to sailing, civil rights to respiratory infections, and prison radio to the 2014 FIFA World Cup, Philippa shows how individuals have the ability to change the way that they – and others – interact with the world around them. A homage to the application of humanity, humility, simplicity and common sense to the pursuit of positive change; it's a uniquely optimistic perspective on business and, more importantly, on life.

—*Jon Steel, Author of 'Truth, Lies and Advertising' and*
'Perfect Pitch'

This is a truly seminal piece of work that not only demonstrates the benefit of a human-to-human approach to business but also highlights the imperative for a different approach to how we operate in the world, where people, the planet and business can all thrive. Every business leader should read and act upon the approach Philippa so brilliantly explains. We must change how we operate for the sake of all humanity and every living being on this planet. It's that important, and this book lays the foundations of how we can achieve it.

—*Chris Norman MBE, Chief Executive Officer, GOOD Agency*

Through master storytelling, Philippa shows us it's time for companies to break the paradigm of profits over people and that at the centre of corporate success is humans. Leaders who put the needs of others before their own, invest in humanity and recognize the organization is bigger than any one person are the ones most likely to reap the greatest returns.

—*Joe Hamrahi, Chief Financial Officer, Highwire Public Relations*

Philippa shares a key message for humanity at this critical time: we need to feel accountable and responsible for the long-term well-being of people and the planet. *Return on Humanity* reminds us that we all have the ingredients and know the recipe to tackle this crisis.

—*Luca Zerbini, Chief Executive Officer and Co-founder, Una Terra Venture Capital Impact Fund*

Philippa offers accessible, practical suggestions for unlocking our human potential at work, helping us realize the immense power we each have to transform companies and society simply by reconnecting with our own humanity. *Return on Humanity* will leave you feeling hopeful and reignite your faith in business as a force for good.

—*David Webster, Co-founder and Chief Executive Officer, The Carrot Collective*

This book makes a clear and compelling argument for harnessing our humanity to create better leaders and enduring change. It is an elegant tapestry of inspiring personal observations, vivid anecdotes and convincing case studies from all over the world. It's a book for people who care. It's a book for now.

—*Jim Carroll, Brand Strategist, Carroll Jones LLP*

This is a brilliant read for anyone open to building bridges. In a fractured world with growing inequalities, finding ways to bridge and collaborate with others outside of your circle is not just a way to uncover common cause. It is a way to discover your own humanity.

—*Ed Mayo, Chief Executive Officer, Pilotlight*

Organizations are run by people, serve people and affect people's lives. But they are often inhuman. Weird. *Return on Humanity* is the antidote. Through simple, inspirational stories and practical guidance, Philippa brings together decades of learning from many cultures and leaders, creating a wonderfully entertaining and compelling narrative. This is a book to change the world one leader at a time. If you're human, a leader and you care about your impact, read it now!

—Charlie Dawson, Founder, The Foundation

PHILIPPA J. WHITE

RETURN
ON

Leadership lessons from all
corners of the world

First published in Great Britain by Practical Inspiration Publishing, 2024

© Philippa J. White, 2024

The moral rights of the author have been asserted

ISBN   9781788605830 (HB)
ISBN   9781788605212 (PB)
ISBN   9781788605236 (epub)
ISBN   9781788605229 (mobi)

Every effort has been made to trace copyright holders and to obtain their permission for the use of copyright material. The publisher apologizes for any errors or omissions and would be grateful if notified of any corrections that should be incorporated in future reprints or editions of this book.

Want to bulk-buy copies of this book for your team and colleagues? We can customize the content and co-brand *Return on Humanity* to suit your business's needs.

Please email info@practicalinspiration.com for more details.

Practical Inspiration
Publishing

For Bia and Maya

In loving memory of my Dad, my Uncle Neil and Jeremy

Contents

Foreword   xv

Introduction: A leader driven by his humanity   xvii

Section 1: Finding your humanity   1

Chapter 1: The special human ingredients   3
Creating connections   3
Flexibility and adaptability starting young   6
Checking egos at the door   7
My way or the highway   9
A shift to connection and belonging   10
Cultural intelligence and collaboration   11
The ripple effect and our dependence on others   13

Chapter 2: What liberates our human assets?   17
The power of disrupting zones of comfort   17
The power of wonder   19
The power of constraints   20
The power of perseverance with passion   22
The power of a positive mindset   24
The power of lived experience   27
The power of a beginner's mind   29

Chapter 3: The impact of using human assets   31
The impact of compassion and agency   31
The impact of empathy   33
The impact of self-awareness and living a life with intention   34
The impact of following your inner compass   36

The impact of resilience   38
The impact of expanding perspectives   39

Section 2: Creating more human leaders and companies   43

Chapter 4: The problem with old business paradigms   45
What if the main goal of business isn't to just make money?   45
What if hiring good humans is more important than just leaders?   49
What if companies choose to be at the service of their people?   51
What if business as usual is failing to benefit everyone?   53

Chapter 5: How a company becomes more human   57
Fostering relationships   57
Having a north star that resonates with people   61
Creating a happy working climate   63
Creating the space to empower others   64
Trusting the strength of difference   65
Celebrating egoless leadership and a shared purpose   68

Chapter 6: The gold dust hidden in the outside-in perspective   71
Placing real people in the driver's seat   71
Treating the planet as another customer   76

Chapter 7: The human stories behind corporate successes   79
Bringing out the best in leaders   79
Being a purpose-driven business: from humans to humans   83
Being in business to save the home planet   86
Forging long-lasting relationships over short-term efficiency   89
Putting humanity at the heart of design   91

Section 3: The outcome of the return on humanity   95

Chapter 8: Creating the necessary conditions for magic to happen   97
The power of integrating humanity into the financial equation   97
The power of forging unlikely partnerships   99
The power of reintegrating people into society   101
The power of building mutually beneficial relationships   103

Chapter 9: The world is a global village, and we are all responsible for its future   105
Becoming consciously aware that local problems are not isolated issues   105
Leveraging the power of the private sector   110
Bringing out the best of people through accountability   114
Shrinking divides to make the world more human   117

Chapter 10: The opportunities out there waiting to be embraced   121
Creating ripples of possibility   121
Lessons from a hummingbird   124
A final challenge   127
An invitation   131

Author's notes   133

Acknowledgements   135

Notes   137

Index   153

Foreword

Philippa White has written a wise and useful book. Its lessons are helpful for those of us who work at Patagonia. I'm happy that all of us who want to do business responsibly now have this book to turn to for inspiration and guidance.

Thirty years ago, Patagonia learned (accidentally by the way) how harmful cotton grown with pesticides is to the soil, the air, local wildlife and human health. We stopped buying conventional cotton and switched entirely to organic fibre purchased directly from farmers – inadvertently casting ourselves outside the known universe of sportswear production. The farmers knew no spinners who turned fibre into yarn. We didn't know any either, having relied on agents who bought cotton by the bale on the commodity market and looked after the process from there.

Spinners didn't want to talk to us. They said they hated organic cotton; it gummed up their machinery. We'd nearly given up (which would have put an end to Patagonia's sportswear line, a third of the business) when Johnny Yeung, who ran one of the largest spinning mills in the world, decided he would try to help. He found that by cooling the temperature on the mill's floor, his machines could spin the organic cotton without breaking down. One business saved.

Years later, we asked Johnny, 'You were so big and our order was so small. Why did you even talk to us?' He thought for a moment, then said, 'I guess you could call me a closet environmentalist.'

Philippa at one point in *Return on Humanity* recounts her experience as a business student attending a lecture in an auditorium as some of her fellow students day-traded on their laptops, fist pumping or quietly yelping when they made a quick profit. The professor, to regain their attention, interrupted his talk to ask, 'What's the main goal of business?' To which the students were expected to chant, and did, 'TO MAKE MONEY!'

But Philippa shows the reader, as Johnny Yeung once showed Patagonia, that business as an activity is as morally engaging and demanding as any other – and can be as meaningful and rewarding.

In our time, material needs for a third of the population in the human world have been more than met, but it is still a profound social pain and conflict between rich and poor. And the harm done to nature, of which we're a part, puts us and so many other species of life in existential peril.

There is no way out of this, but there may still be a way through; one that relies not on the escape by a few from the fate (and threat) of the many but with the help of guardian angels inherent in human nature. Despair or cynicism certainly won't rescue us, neither will hope of deliverance by magical means. But a sense of agency is essential; what Haisla leader Gerald Amos called the most important right humans have – the right (not the obligation) to be responsible. This is not entirely altruism. Patagonia's halls are filled with part-time athletes, and like Philippa who was a competitive rower, they all know that no one can win, even against yourself, without some form of cooperation with others. The core of this book is its illustration of the spirit and different forms of cooperation that make possible what people might regard, beforehand, as impossible. These include the cultivation of a sense of wonder, a way to view the inside of an enterprise from the outside looking in and an acceptance, sometimes an embrace, of constraints that force us to think – and allow us to act – in a new way.

The author, who is the founder and CEO of a consultancy firm called TIE, was born in South Africa, has lived in Canada and the UK and is a long-time resident of Brazil. It is refreshing to read stories of productive behaviour not set in predictable high-rise business districts or business-park settings but in enterprises around the world including Brazil, the US, Canada, Tanzania, Malawi, Zambia and South Africa, where human resourcefulness outstrips the limited resources available. This leads to some interesting observations you're not likely to find in other business books, especially those that centre on leadership, motivation and culture. Check out the exercise called 'Elephant, Dead Fish and Vomit.'

Return on Humanity does cover the ground on how to make a business succeed as a money-maker through enlivening its people and culture. But much more than that, it shows how enlivening can help a business be a force for social and ecological good, which in the long run, turns out to be the same thing. Its tales from the corners of the world are key to this. I loved an antidote to received wisdom (and convenient pessimism) delivered by the Dalai Lama: 'Nothing exists as it appears.'

My favourite though comes from Alejandro Jodorowsky: 'Birds born in a cage think flying is an illness.' It's time for us all to step outside, and work outside, our cages. To realize our agency and capacity for cooperative purpose is to make use of the ways in which we are still healthy. We need to build on that if we are to heal our world.

Vincent Stanley, Director of Philosophy, Patagonia

Introduction: A leader driven by his humanity

As I looked around the crowded room, I saw a sea of expectant faces.

A few weeks before, my Uncle Neil had died peacefully in his home following a short illness. I remember being blown away by the diversity of people who attended his celebration of life that day in 2004.

Among them, medical colleagues from South Africa, family from around the world, friends, trade unionists and activists from apartheid struggle days – some who by then were members of South Africa's new democratic parliament.

Growing up, Neil was always a huge inspiration to me. Although I was born in South Africa, I didn't have as much contact with him as I would have liked, as we moved to Canada when I was three years old. But the stories he told us when we visited him in Cape Town had a huge impact on my life.

As a physician and occupational health specialist, he had dedicated his life to working against the injustices and inequalities in the apartheid health system.[1] He talked about the challenges of the medical system in a racially divided and deeply unequal country, and his public health practice and research focused on occupational health risks in the South African textiles and mining industries. He also provided voluntary and sometimes clandestine medical support to political activists during the height of the anti-apartheid struggle in the 1980s.

Neil was always so humble and there was one story that almost never came up – but one I was so enamoured by: the time he worked closely with Nelson Mandela, or to him, Madiba.

When the first round of negotiations following the release of Mandela in 1990 took place between the African National Congress (ANC) and the apartheid government, the ANC was asked to select a physician to be present. While Neil was never a member of any political party, he was active in the National Medical and Dental Association (NAMDA), an affiliate of the United Democratic Front (UDF), as a trusted health activist and highly experienced physician, so was asked to provide this service.[2,3] He formed part of the support team who were present, day and night, throughout the first round of negotiations with the apartheid government. Neil was trusted implicitly to ensure that Mandela stayed healthy and well during these negotiations.

According to my Aunt, Neil took several photos during this time. Many of the ANC leadership, including Mandela, featured in these photos, along with the ANC support team. However, there isn't one photo of Neil with Mandela. He never wanted a show or saw the necessity to put the spotlight on himself. He always just quietly got on with what he thought was important, and that was enough.

Various family members, friends and colleagues spoke at the celebration of Neil's life in 2004. Others spoke too, and it was their input that compelled me to do what I do now, and to write this book.

When the planned tributes had finished, a man sitting in the row behind me put up his hand and asked to speak. He told us he was from a community in Cape Town where few people spoke English, so medical help was always difficult; few doctors at the time spoke the local language. Neil was one of the very few doctors in the public health system who had learned isiXhosa, and the man said he would never forget how this was appreciated by the patients who came to the clinic.[4]

It made me wonder how other doctors effectively treated patients without being able to communicate with them.

Next, a woman talked about Neil's unwavering commitment during the dark days of apartheid. She was Zo Kota, a young activist during the 1980s who was involved in women and student organizations. She shared how Neil treated youth and apartheid struggle veterans who were either too scared or too ill to get to government clinics. Often, he was taking great risks to do this.[5]

Then, another woman put up her hand: Lizzie Phike. My Aunt later told me she was a veteran trade unionist from the food sector. She had a powerful presence and confidently strode to the front of the room where she told a moving story about how Neil gave her support at a very difficult time in her life. In the 1980s, during one of the states of emergency, trade unionist and community activists were placed in detention due to their involvement in the apartheid struggle. This was a terrifying experience. People were held in solitary cells in police stations for periods of up to six months, with no access to lawyers or family. Lizzie was held in detention in a small town near Cape Town and needed medical help. Neil was one of a group of progressive doctors who assisted whenever they could. She said that Neil, without fail, visited her while she remained in detention and was able to give her news of what was happening on the outside. 'He was the light at a very dark time in my life,' she said. I think I was holding my breath the whole time she spoke.

As I listened to everyone who had stories to tell about my Uncle that day, I started to reflect on why Neil was so inspirational to me. What was it that captured the room's attention? What made him touch so many people's lives? Why was this gathering to celebrate his life full of so many people from various backgrounds?

I realized the reason why Neil had such a profound impact on all of us was because of his humanity; he had centred his life and purpose around it completely. It was also his endless fascination with perspective and possibility. He wasn't a typical White South African doctor, especially at a time when South Africa was run by a horribly oppressive apartheid regime. He spent time connecting with people in professions and backgrounds different to his own. He had a deeply felt sense of responsibility and commitment to human values, and his purpose and human compass were directly related to impacting others. He was humble, authentic, totally driven by a sense of purpose, and he went out of his way to challenge the status quo in numerous ways over the years.

Returning to my day job in London, I started to reflect on the day-to-day reality of my life and the silo that I found myself in.

I started to think of the people I worked with, our daily routines and the exposure that many of us had to people outside our frames of reference. We lived in a middle-class, Soho bubble. We worked hard, mostly with people from a similar background, went to the pub in Soho after work to let off steam – also surrounded by people from comparable social groups – and lived with people who we either knew before or were like-minded. Yet, we were expected to give nuanced advice to clients, build global brands, think bigger and effectively lead teams. I realized that was only possible if we had the opportunity to step across divides, expand our minds, introduce discomfort and expose ourselves to different realities. It's only then that we could become more relatable, more informed and better advisors.

If being an inspirational and impactful leader required these types of opportunities, how were we ever to develop the leaders our companies and world needed?

I started to think about the leaders I connected with and the people I looked up to. They had ideas beyond their own world, were interested and interesting, cared for and understood others, and were open-minded and flexible. They were courageous enough to challenge the status quo, took calculated risks and embraced discomfort. They were able to respond in uncertain, complex and ambiguous circumstances. I realized it was the leaders who invested in their humanity that stood out and had what it took to drive their teams, companies and the world in the right direction.

I then started to reflect on the state of the world and realized that many businesses had become machines, forgetting that it's the humans that they have hired that make them successful and viable. They've also lost their connection with society and the environment. We have scarcity of supply, serious challenges with climate change and biodiversity, and civil society is no longer accepting that business can't do anything about all of this.

Companies are struggling to hire and retain employees, and people are looking for motivation, connection and meaning in what they do, wanting to feel free and alive. This is about companies outbehaving the competition. Not in the traditional sense of growth, cost cutting or certain marketing tactics. I am talking about businesses ensuring that they make all their stakeholders feel good in every aspect of what they do.

I've always believed that businesses can be a force for good and fundamental to the solution to create a fairer world, although many aren't built to make it that right now. It's the more human organizations that will not only impact the world but are proven to be more competitive; but they don't just happen. The prerequisite to being a human company are leaders that have tapped into their humanity.

The science is clear. We still have six years to prevent irreversible damage from climate change.[6] However, if we don't do something, life on this planet is going to get so much worse than we think. But change is possible, and the power to do something about all of this is in our hands.

Considering the state of the world, I created a company in 2006 that didn't merely refine leadership – the idea was to totally refocus it.

For two decades I've been helping leaders engage with their humanity to create more competitive and impactful businesses. I have done this through the creation of experiential leadership programmes that foster self-aware, thoughtful leaders who inspire successful enterprises; and my close collaboration with the world's top-tier companies has transformed millions of lives globally. My company works in 26 countries around the world, connects various sectors, and through the programmes, I've made it my mission to create better people, which lead to better companies, and then a better world.

In the following pages I intend to bring my thinking about humanity, and my learnings over the past two decades working in business, to life.

This is a human business book. You'll find examples drawn not only from the world of business, but also from the wider, infinitely more interesting world of human experience. Expect detailed stories from different sectors around the world that illustrate the transformative power of people's greatest asset – their humanity.

However, before I go any further, let me share my definition of 'human', which has two parts. First, it's being aware of how we all fit together, and I break this down into three areas:

○ **Self-awareness**: Being true to who you are, fully aware of what fulfils you, and in touch with your strengths and weaknesses. It's so easy to think we need to be someone else, do things like other people or work towards the expectations of others. But in fact, the key is remembering that power lies in who we are and truly understanding who that person is. Once we have that clarity, we are free to be genuinely purposeful.

o **Interconnectedness**: We must never forget that everything is linked. A decision made in one place can impact another, either directly or indirectly, and for better or worse.

o **Interdependence**: It's remembering how interdependent we are. We depend on others for our well-being or reaching a desired objective, and it's damaging to underestimate the importance of collaboration, of citizenship and our role in the wider world.

For the above to be possible we need to behave in a certain way, and this leads me to the second part of my definition: we can't forget that the 'softer' attributes of kindness and compassion are as important as everything on the balance sheet, and I see these as human assets.

Throughout the book I will also draw on other human assets of flexibility, adaptability, cultural intelligence, humility, vulnerability and empathy, making the point that the 21st century businessperson can't overlook these powerful forces.

The book is divided into three sections, which focus on three distinct realities – individuals, companies and the world – and I will discuss human assets within the context of each reality. I also see each one building on the other.

o **Section 1 – Individuals:** I first focus on the importance of seeing ourselves as individuals before we see ourselves as leaders. We are people first. No matter your role, the money you have or where you live, we are all human. It's in our daily lives that we discover our power to connect, understand, listen and open our minds. This section sets the stage, and the stories illustrate what can happen when individuals tap into the human assets that we all have access to. Once we get this right, the rest follows.

o **Section 2 – Companies:** Next, I bring this thinking into the business world. I argue for more humanity in the development and application of leadership and include numerous stories and proof points from various business leaders around the world, illustrating that companies are more competitive when they are human centred.

o **Section 3 – The World:** Finally, the third section illustrates how more human leaders create the ripples to bring the change needed for a more sustainable planet and a better world for us all.

My intention in this book is not to be prescriptive; I prefer to share observations about what I have learned working with various people, businesses and leaders around the world over the last 20 years. I also believe that we can learn from everyone, everywhere; we all have something important to offer and teach. Neither is this an anti-business book. Instead, I aim to show you there is another way.

This is not a radical rethink, but instead a refocus and readjustment of expertise and resources from the commercial world to be slanted more towards improving the planet and the people within it. I long for a world where we broaden our collective capacities, encourage self-worth and care for others as much as bottom lines and returns.

Return on Humanity is the payback of being more human, of honing the behaviours, attitudes and conventional mindsets of leaders in business. It's the consequence of better interactions between people and more thoughtful leadership that starts to shift cultures within the workplace, leading to better companies and positively impacting the world we live in.

So, thank you for joining me, and I look forward to having you on this journey.

Section 1
Finding your humanity

A few stories bringing to life the human assets to tap into, how to unleash them and what it looks like when you do.

1

The special human ingredients

Kindness is one of the greatest superpowers in the world, as is humility. Another one is to be vulnerable, which demonstrates courage and takes strength, and participation and connection are key in any relationship to build trust.

The following stories in the first three chapters are rooted in human interaction and daily life. Specifically in this chapter, I will identify the necessary human assets, help to bring to life the importance of them, how they are intrinsic to all of us and how they make our daily interactions so much more successful when we unlock them.

From Chapter 4 onwards, I will then take these human assets, the foundational building blocks, and illustrate their power in leadership and business.

But for now, here are some stories to bring to life my thinking.

Creating connections

Depending on where you are in the world, you may not know that in Canada every province's licence plate has a slogan that sums up that province. There is *Beautiful British Columbia*, *Wild Rose Country* (for Alberta) and *Friendly Manitoba*. I grew up in *Friendly Manitoba*.

For anyone that knows Manitoba, it's a tough place to live. It's -45°C in the winter, -60°C with the windchill, so life logistics when it's cold aren't easy. Walking to school requires a ridiculous number of clothes, you need to plug your car in before you walk into the house to ensure the car heater will warm up your car ready for the morning, and driving on roads full of ice and snow requires real skill.

But despite the challenges, and the human tendency to stay inside when it's that cold outside, the sense of community and relationships in Manitoba are second to none. I understand how we have this sense of community in a place like the northeast of Brazil, where I've lived since 2007, as it's hot all year round. As a result, society has had time throughout the year, every year, to develop relationships and that cultural and community fabric. But it's interesting that Manitoba has not only managed to acquire the name 'Friendly Manitoba' in such a frigid climate six months a year, but also lives and breathes it authentically all year round.

One of the most fundamental elements to being human is connectedness and relationships. We are inherently social creatures and we want to belong, for the most part thriving in social groups. As the world becomes ever more complex, being socially connected becomes even more important. Strong ties with the community provide us with happiness, security and support, and our mental and physical health improves because of these connections. This genuine human contact can even protect us against anxiety and depression. Communities and people who understand this power are providing that necessary protective social fabric; and Manitoba figured that out.

Tapping into the power of connectedness has incredible strength. Before I studied a business degree in Ontario ('Yours to discover' as the province's licence plate says), I did a couple of years at the University of Winnipeg, one of Manitoba's main universities, studying history, economics, sociology, psychology and my favourite, conflict resolution studies. These two years were key for me. They were the start of my personal journey to understand what it takes to really tap into human assets, what it looks like when this isn't happening and what happens when someone's humanity is ignited.

Over the years I realized that the building blocks for becoming an impactful leader start with understanding ourselves as individuals and discovering our individual power to connect and relate to others. The first time that I became aware of this was in my first year at the University of Winnipeg in 1997; my professor of conflict resolution left an indelible mark on my soul. She was an unassuming woman whose husband joined her in a neighbouring classroom to look after their young baby (if I remember correctly, she was still breastfeeding). One day, she told us a story that I don't think I'll ever forget.

When she was travelling in Guatemala at the start of the 1990s, a time when the country was still immersed in a civil war and a few years before she became a professor, she was captured by the guerrillas. The odds weren't great for her to leave unscarred. One day, while she was talking with the people who captured her, she started to make balloon animals. The simple and quite insignificant gesture was enough to reframe the relationship with her captors. Instead of being seen as a prisoner and an enemy, she suddenly became another human being, like them. That was enough to create a bond and a different connection, which then developed a relationship between her and the guards. Eventually, she was set free.

When she told us this story, for the first time I understood the tremendous power of this type of connection, and a more human way of doing things as a driving force to achieve a desired outcome. By tapping into her human assets, she used her ability of connection to win over the guards. She proved the power of relating to others and creating a common connection and understanding. She turned a conflict into a win–win situation simply by being more human.

This story illustrates how a simple human gesture, even in the most extreme or dire circumstances, can turn things around. She had the wisdom and strength to approach her captors as people. Imagine a leader who has the same ability to tap into their inner strength and approach situations that go beyond status or roles and acknowledge a common humanity before anything else. It's this skill that can turn any extreme situation into one where everyone wins. We'll talk more about this in Section 2.

The sense of community at the University of Winnipeg was also high. There was little ego, people were there to learn together and I always felt supported by the students and the professors. In each class, we had buddies that we could rely on to help us with writing notes. If the professor talked quickly and said something that we missed, you could always rely on a table buddy to fill in the blanks. We helped each other, and we were all stronger for it.

The challenge was when I went to business school in Ontario. I'll never forget how things changed, what it looks like when these human values aren't there and when that simple and authentic connectedness is absent. I remember sitting beside someone in class in a similar situation to that in Winnipeg, writing notes as the professor spoke. Only now we had computers, rather than paper and pens, and we were marked on a bell curve. When I got left behind and asked my table buddy for help, rather than turning the computer to show the notes, she turned the computer in a way that blocked me from seeing anything. Suddenly things were very different.

As Dorothy from the Wizard of Oz said, 'Toto, I've a feeling we're not in Kansas anymore.'

I was no longer surrounded by a supportive and compassionate community. Quite the contrary. I was entering a world of savage competition, bell curves and ego. I wondered if I was starting to get an insight into the world of business. What I did know was that I wasn't in 'Friendly Manitoba' anymore.

Seeing that stark contrast was important, and it clearly demonstrated two very different cultures. The University of Winnipeg fostered a feeling of connection, community and belonging, and we all thrived as a result. We enjoyed being there and did well. Stepping into the world of business at the university in Ontario was a shock, but I started to recognize that competition and ego-driven leadership is a choice. I saw that it leads to feelings of insecurity and anxiety, and I personally didn't feel as though it was an environment where I could thrive. If we want to lead other people, communities or businesses, what are the outcomes we are looking for?

Flexibility and adaptability starting young

'Practice early who wants to become a master.'

German proverb[1]

A little over a year ago a family brought this proverb to life, showing me in real time what outcomes are possible when you start seeking the powerful skills of flexibility, adaptability and resilience in children. Even if it means pushing them in new ways and out of their zones of comfort.

The family is made up of an American mum and a Brazilian father who met in Italy. The children were born in Italy and speak Italian, English and Portuguese. When I met them, the children were eight and ten years of age, and they had started a three-year round the world sailing journey. They set off from Europe, stopped in Cape Verde, and we met in the northeast of Brazil as they started to make their way down to the tip of South America for the first major leg of their adventure.

It may feel extreme for some, but travelling around the world has made these children so flexible and adaptable to uncomfortable situations. They have adjusted to their home schooling aboard, eat absolutely everything, they can talk to anyone and can amuse themselves for hours. They are not only adaptable, but also empathetic, kind and extremely resilient. The unstructured reality of sailing, where so many unexpected situations arise from one moment to the other, has allowed these children to internalize these human skills very quickly. By travelling thousands of miles at a time crossing continents, they've had to regularly learn to adjust to new realities.

We all have human assets, and we can choose to access them or not. Sometimes it's easy to forget they are there, or we unconsciously keep them dormant, but these parents made the decision to make these children consciously aware of these skills and they use them every day. Through the constant exposure to different languages, cultures and routines, their human assets have been awakened, and they've learned to thrive, even in the face of adversity. It's important experiences and learning opportunities like these that will develop the necessary tools that, without question, they'll carry into adulthood and be the leaders that the world needs now. Other families have seen the value in this too.[2]

'Flexible thinking is the ability to think about things in a new or different way. It helps us deal with uncertainty, solve problems, adjust to changes and incorporate new information into our plans and ideas.'

Rae Jacobson, the Child Mind Institute[3]

Parents of adaptable children know that flexibility is a skill and both lead to more resilience. Psychologists view flexibility as a neurocognitive skill that develops over time and the more parents can gift their children with these future proofing abilities, the more resilient and capable they will be as adults.

Flexibility and adaptability are not, unfortunately, intrinsic to us, but the capacity is there to learn and turn them into habitual behaviours. Perhaps by awakening that child in us, we can be better suited to deal with uncertainty and chaos and become comfortable despite the complexities we face in this world.

Checking egos at the door

'We do not see things as they are.
We see things as we are.'

Anaïs Nin[4]

There are many global international development organizations around the world that have various missions to help people in the Global South and work to address the social and environmental complexities faced. However, many times, decisions are made in one place, and then executed in another, and often don't involve the people on the ground. Here is an example of this phenomenon, which unfortunately is very common.

Everyone wants to have water closer to home – or do they? A few years ago, a well was installed in the centre of a local community in Malawi. However, the well kept breaking and no one could understand why. After weeks, and possibly even months, passed, the local community decided to install video cameras to discover what on earth was happening. It turned out to be the same woman, time and time again, breaking the well. When they asked her why she was doing it, her response was so revealing. She was being abused in her home. Collecting water was her only excuse to leave the house and be amongst her friends. Once the well was installed, she no longer had a reason to go out, and without that outlet, she was essentially a prisoner in her own house.

The well was installed with the greatest of intentions, but one decision made in one place had knock-on effects in another. As Anaïs Nin said, people tend to see the world not as it is, but as they are. Whatever decision anyone makes, however people try and help, it is always wise to first remember to ask questions, and truly try and understand the local context by actively listening to the answers.

This is clearly a complex situation; of course, the local community would prefer to have water close to home. But before any intervention, there are usually other issues that need to be considered which aren't immediately evident to outsiders because they aren't easily heard or easily spoken about; it's important to be able to read between the lines. If those subtleties aren't understood, the impact from stepping in may not always be positive, be it directly or indirectly.

It takes time to understand complex contexts, and the nuanced conversations often need to be had in more delicate ways; it's never a one-size-fits-all solution to unearth different realities. Although not easy, opening one's eyes to see a perspective from another person's point of view, working *with* people and not doing to them, and taking the time to truly understand the ripple effects of any intervention are the most powerful and effective ways to connect and to build trust with people.

In the business world, there are no doubt similar situations that most of us have experienced at one time or another. Moments when we have railroaded a conversation, or when we haven't stopped to fully take on board someone's comments and ideas. On reflection, there are probably things that could have been done differently, and it most likely comes down to how we showed up. It's so important for us to notice patterns of behaviours that derail us from being our best. It may be to remember to take that extra minute to slow down, perhaps make the effort to bring other departments into the decision-making processes, or simply ask more questions to develop more trust between us and another group of people.

Ernesto Sirolli brings this to life further in his TED talk watched close to four million times, 'Want to help someone? Shut up and Listen.'[5] He touches on a time in Africa that shaped his career, not dissimilar to the story I mentioned above. Ernesto found himself in Zambia and he came across a group of well-intentioned Italians that were keen to teach Zambian people how to grow food. They arrived with Italian seeds in southern Zambia in a beautiful valley that stretched to the Zambezi River, and they started to teach the local people how to grow Italian tomatoes, zucchinis and other vegetables.

The thing was that the local people really weren't interested, and the Italians couldn't understand why. It was such a fertile valley and nothing was being grown. Ernesto tells us that in the Italians' minds, the Zambians were really missing out. But instead of asking why there was no agriculture being grown, or trying to understand the local reality, they just simply thought, as Ernesto said, 'Thank God we're here. Just in the nick of time to save the Zambian people from starvation.'[6]

He continues to tell the story of how everything grew beautifully, demonstrating to the Zambians just how easy it all was, and how lucky they were to have this input.

Until one fateful day when it all became clear. When all the food was ready to eat, beautiful red tomatoes and gorgeous zucchinis, 200 hippos came out from the river and ate everything.

'My God, the hippos!' exclaimed the Italians.

'Yes, that's why we have no agriculture here,' said the Zambians.

'Why didn't you tell us?' asked the Italians.

'Because you never asked,' replied the Zambians.

This story is so powerful. You see, with any of these types of interventions, participation is so key and trust needs to be built. We can't expect people to tell us what they think if they aren't included from the beginning. The solutions need to be created together. The lack of trust and collaboration from the beginning meant the Zambians didn't feel a part of this initiative.

No matter how much someone wants to help or implement something new, they first need to create connection. This is done by asking questions and then listening to the answers; reading between the lines, hearing what is *not* being said and listening to the differences. It's a good idea to check egos at the door, have conversations where one truly starts to understand the other person's reality, and abandon the belief that one person has all the answers.

My way or the highway

> 'Doubt is not a pleasant condition,
> but certainty is absurd.'
>
> *Voltaire[7]*

To be able to unpick new realities and truly understand someone else certainly requires an ability to actively listen and be humble, but equally people need to tap into the power of vulnerability and reflection. People need to invest the time to take on opinions of others. This not only demonstrates that they don't think they have all the answers, but also acknowledges that having all the solutions would probably be impossible if working with people from other backgrounds that they know nothing about, as the story above suggests.

This is the virtue of questioning your certainty, and sometimes even your expertise. Not an easy thing to do when people are usually in the driver's seat and used to being in positions of power. People who are brilliant in one area are not necessarily competent in another, and this overconfidence is a trap of being an expert.[8]

It can be hard to let go and express vulnerability, but when you allow yourself not to have complete certainty about something, your ability to reflect is greater. Your mind opens, you have more vision and the world around you gets bigger. In the modern, fast-changing business world, more than ever, it's the people in power that need to demonstrate humility and vulnerability. This creates more connection with those around them, fosters better working relationships and opens the door to more information.

Brené Brown brings this to life through her research. She identified that what 'full-hearted' people have in common is a sense of courage; courage to simply be imperfect.[9] These people can admit mistakes and failings and ask opinions from those 'below' them. I consider 'full-hearted' people those who have tapped into the power of their human assets, which includes vulnerability and humility.

Brené found that these people are fully able to embrace vulnerability and believe that what makes them vulnerable makes them beautiful. In her research, they didn't talk about vulnerability as being comfortable, nor did they talk about it being excruciating. They just talked about it being necessary to live in a more human way.

This is about marrying courage with vulnerability and showing up with all our weaknesses and strengths. Once we master this in our everyday encounters, it's then much easier to do it in a business environment, which I'll go into more detail in Section 2.

A shift to connection and belonging

Strong leadership relies on a sense of belonging and a solid foundation of connection with others. This connection takes time, vulnerability and courage. But another ingredient is also important.

A few years ago, I was interviewed over Zoom by a class of children in Canada ranging from six to eleven years of age. It was probably one of the most revealing interviews I've ever had.

The talk was about daring to explore different places, and I explained that when people do that, they grow. I talked about the power of meeting new people and establishing friendships with children different to them. I went on to explain how enriching all of this can be because we learn new words, try unfamiliar foods and discover different ways of doing things, which makes life so much more fun. We also start to truly understand what other people are going through and how they are feeling. I explained that everyone needs to have these types of experiences, both children and adults.

I then started to tell stories of my work that involves children from other parts of the world, their realities and what we do to help them; this was when things got interesting. It was at this point that the children started to lean into the camera. But what was even more fascinating was what happened next.

My youngest, who was six at the time, came and sat on my lap at the end of the interview, and I explained that she speaks Portuguese as we are in Brazil. At that point, a little boy who was quiet the entire time and hidden in the back of the group promptly ran to the camera, forgot that he was shy, and started talking to her in Portuguese.

The connection through a shared language awakened that child. Who would have thought that such a spontaneous, unexpected moment would have had such an impact on that little boy who until then hadn't been engaging with the conversation or with the rest of the group. This common humanity was the key to unlocking his courage and interest and fostered that sense of belonging.

This is the power of a shared experience. It changes how you see yourself, others around you and the world. It's often natural moments like these that happen when people are courageous enough to share a space with others who are different to them, and these moments can occur in the most unexpected ways. They help create bridges with others, develop feelings of belonging, connectedness and a sense of meaning. These commonalities across borders, whether they be geographical, cultural or generational, show us that we are all more similar than we think and that we long for the same things, even though we come from different generations, cultures and backgrounds.

People love to feel a sense of belonging, no matter their age, and so the more we can truly surrender to this power and help others find those opportunities to discover shared interests, beliefs and values, the deeper and more meaningful friendships, partnerships and professional relationships will be created. Shared experiences are important for leaders looking to form high-performing teams as they help people bond, allowing them to work better together. I will talk more about this in the context of the corporate world in Section 2.

Cultural intelligence and collaboration

As the issues facing the world become increasingly complex, we all need to be able to adapt across different boundaries to create important bonds with others. The people who will be the most successful doing this are those who will cross and connect cultures, who understand multiple worlds and resonate with people different from themselves.

Although I live in Brazil, I return to London a few times a year for meetings. In 2023, after a full-day session with a client, I stepped out on Great Portland Street looking for something quick to eat. I was hungry and needed something easy to grab before heading to my next meeting. Across the street, I saw a take-away Thai restaurant, and it was exactly what I fancied. I went in and was greeted by two friendly people.

Having lived in Thailand for about six months while I finished my business degree on exchange, I not only fell in love with the country, but also learned some idiosyncrasies from the culture that have stuck with me ever since. As I waited for my food, I started chatting with the people behind the counter. Very quickly we shared stories of Bangkok, of the area where I lived and shared common experiences. As I left, I thanked them in their language. Nothing huge happened that afternoon, but the experience was so much more than a simple exchange of food for money, and we all left positively impacted as a result.

Our daily lives are full of opportunities like this one where we can be exposed to other cultures, subcultures and generations. There are parts of cities that have attracted groups of people from another country, new neighbours may have moved in with a teenage son that likes to listen to an unfamiliar genre of music, or we may have new in-laws to adjust to and understand. We also work in companies with various departments, full of people with different skill sets and backgrounds. Whatever it is, we are constantly being asked to cross borders and find commonalities to relate to others. The people who can do that comfortably, spontaneously and authentically have started to develop their human asset of cultural intelligence (CQ), and this only happens when people go out into the world, talk to others and exchange experiences; not just have them.

In her book *Cultural Intelligence: CQ: The Competitive Edge for Leaders Crossing Borders*, Julia Middleton explains that CQ is the natural evolution from the now well-established notions of intelligence quotient (IQ) and emotional intelligence (EQ).[10] CQ is considered an essential ingredient for leaders who recognize that they can no longer work in a vacuum.

The world requires that people have CQ now more than ever. We need it to function comfortably across cultural borders, operate effectively in unfamiliar surroundings and find ways to break down barriers that aren't always only geographical. To spark innovation and find the solutions to the difficulties that our world faces, we need to be able to work across sectors, network better, gain trust from people who are unlike ourselves and relate to different generations. We need to be able to see a wider context when looking at a challenge or running a project, and this is only possible by involving others from outside of our frames of reference. And to do this, people must have CQ.

Once CQ has been acquired, it's a fantastic, nuanced understanding of someone's unfamiliar and ambiguous gestures; the same way that people from that local culture would understand them. This is not just about crossing boundaries; it's being able to understand what's happening when we get there.

More than ever, we need people who can identify with situations that are different to what they are used to, people who actively seek out these opportunities and are able to inspire people to come together to solve challenges and make progress. CQ has everything to do with making all of this possible.

The ripple effect and our dependence on others

'Your greatness is measured by your horizons.'

Michelangelo[11]

Shifts are taking place that call for each one of us to understand our global interdependence and it's the people who have CQ, who understand multiple worlds and can cross and connect these cultures, that will not only thrive, but be sought after. They are the ones that can unpick what they have been doing forever, laugh at their mistakes and embrace difference in order to better understand how the world works and involve others to help find solutions.

No problem, anywhere, can be solved by one person, one country, one sector or one company. We need one another to not only understand the subtleties and intricacies of the various challenges we face, but to also find the innovative solutions. Yet, most people spend the majority of their time operating within the boundaries of their comfortable silos. The lack of perspective diminishes information available and leaves people with little understanding of the wider world around them.

Dismissing these realities, in some instances, can be seen as insignificant in terms of general impact. In other situations, the consequences are important as they ill-prepare us to deal with problems because we lose out on necessary information that other people, sectors and cultures can teach us. We forget that the world is a deeply interconnected system, where a small occurrence in one place can have a large impact on another.

One example of an insignificant consequence of ignorance is what I experienced when I arrived in Thailand in January 2001, a year after Y2K.

Those of you reading who were alive in the year 2000 and old enough to remember Y2K, which was related to potential computer errors caused by the formatting and storage of calendar data, will no doubt recall the hype.[12] The scare turned into something larger than life and took over conversations and news programmes for months.

When I arrived in Thailand later that year, I remember talking with my Thai university colleagues about the Y2K phenomenon, curious to know what conversations were being had in Thailand leading up to the year 2000, and if they shared the same concerns. Had it reached such a fevered pitch? Even though I was already fairly well-travelled and considered myself to be somewhat open-minded, I had just assumed this was a global experience.

Their answer floored me: you do know that the year is 2544 here, right?

Wow.

Of course it is; they used a different calendar. Although I knew theoretically that the entire world didn't revolve around the Gregorian calendar, I had just assumed that this huge panic was a shared issue; that the way *we* do things is just the way that things are done. I was stuck in my own little world and way of thinking. But this realization, for me, changed the way I saw things forever. It was also the first time I realized that for these kinds of 'aha' moments to happen, we need to seek out opportunities that get us seeing the world, and ourselves, differently.

Life is busy. We might have children to look after, jobs to do, houses to clean and parents to care for. At the end of a long day, we want to comfortably be with those we love and can relate to, go on holiday to a place we know will suit our needs and desires, and it's fun to go to a bar with like-minded people who help us escape from the stresses of life. But these comfortable routines force us into thinking in a certain way. They reinforce our biased perspectives, our fears, beliefs and education, and we end up falling back on assumptions.

My work has me being exposed regularly to global challenges that various people and communities face around the world. Through it, I have seen the energy that comes from stepping out of the status quo and away from the usual dialogues and discourse; how doing this creates more of a critical eye, a desire to push for the full story of a situation and the involvement of all stakeholders. I see how conversations with people from different backgrounds and sectors open new channels of thinking, which then helps to solve problems in new ways.

This global perspective makes us acutely aware of our interconnectedness and interdependence by linking us to others and the environment around us, and many of the organizations I work with around the world provide clear examples that brings this to life through the important work they do.

Consider hurricanes, for example. I'm sure you, like most of us, have heard about the importance of keeping coral reefs healthy as they are critical to the ecological and economic health for global regions around the world. But have you stopped to think about what happens to coral reefs after a hurricane? Who repairs them? What is involved in that repair? And why is the repair of coral reefs so important to cities and coastlines? I personally had never thought about this before I worked with the Meso American Reef Fund (MAR Fund), based in Guatemala.[13] We hear about hurricanes impacting various regions around the Earth and how they are increasing in the face of climate change, but I had never really stopped to think about the other aspects of such disasters.

When there is a hurricane, the first line of defence are the reefs. After a hurricane they are damaged, and organizations like MAR Fund support experienced people to go onto the reefs after hurricanes and repair and restore them so not only the ecosystems can continue to flourish, but they can recover in order to continue their role in protecting communities on the shore.

This information should make all of us stop and think about our behaviours, especially those who live close to a coast. If the first line of defence of the coastlines are the reefs, then there is a clear cause and effect for people to do all they can to look after them. Individual actions that ensure the health of the reefs by not polluting the beaches, for example, or supporting more sustainable tourism that doesn't damage the reefs, ends up directly impacting their well-being. This is the ripple effect of one person's individual actions.

How about deforestation? This is a major issue in Brazil and has been for decades. But what is the cause and how can we help?

The media talked about the former Brazilian president Bolsonaro being a major cause, infamous for significantly contributing to deforestation in the Brazilian Amazon.[14] We also know that beef and soy production are top drivers of deforestation in the world's tropical forests.[15] But there are other major factors that don't make the headlines.

I have partnered with a Brazilian organization called Iracambi for years.[16] They work to protect and restore the Brazilian Atlantic Forest and improve the lives of the people who live there, and they have been doing it for decades. Conversations with the Iracambi team opened my eyes and helped me realize that some of the major challenges related to deforestation are linked to local farmers and their survival. They cut down the trees to grow coffee or plant pasture so that they can put food on the table. Iracambi helped me understand that a major solution to the destruction of the Brazilian Atlantic Forest is education and awareness raising. When the farmers realize that both their land and their livelihoods will benefit significantly if they protect their forest patches, both the forest and the farmers win.

Instead of regarding these farmers as drivers of deforestation, Iracambi includes them as important and necessary agents of restoration. Local community members are seen as valued partners in reforesting their land, strengthening the biodiversity that contributes to enhanced farm productivity and creating a healthier environment for themselves, their families and the larger community.

The advantages of cohesion and collaboration aren't just felt in the world of international development. Leaders, companies and the wider world progress tremendously when people choose to tap into their humanity by creating more fluidity around divisions, industries and networks. To involve others that think differently, or that come from dissimilar backgrounds, is sometimes slower, more complicated and doesn't always go the way we want it to. But often the best solutions come to fruition when we remember that there is strength in difference and when people make an effort to foster unlikely partnerships. I'll bring this to life further in Section 2.

I also work with an organization in the Kurdistan Region of Iraq, Iraq and Syria called Jiyan Foundation for Human Rights who support survivors of human rights violations, defends fundamental freedoms and promotes democratic values.[17] Jiyan Foundation provides psychotherapy and mental health support to trauma survivors, many of whom are survivors of ISIS cruelty. Asmaa Ibrahim M. Salih,

Co-head of Trauma Care and Health at Jiyan Foundation, shared with me that a large part of their mental health work is rooted in developing the self-awareness of their clients.[18]

Self-awareness opens people's eyes to who they are, how their past has developed them into the person who exists now and helps them better understand what their patterns of behaviour and attitudes are towards everything around them. Once someone has clarity about themselves, they can start to respond to things they want to change and live their life with more intention. By encouraging her students to reflect in this way, Asmaa's work provides people with the power to take back control of their lives and thus shape their communities. All of this ultimately works to create more stability in the region.

Jiyan Foundation has shown me the power of self-awareness and the importance of this human asset to fight against such an oppressive regime, but our conversations have also made me reflect on just how much we can learn from people in different parts of the world. If they can help others around Iraq and Syria become more resilient, and work towards creating a more stable region through self-awareness, we can certainly take this into the business environment to create more resilient leaders and more stable companies. Just think of how powerful it would be for leaders to be more in touch with their values and beliefs, ensuring that the decisions they make in all aspects of their lives are ones that fulfil them. I'll bring this to life further in the next two sections of the book.

These new perspectives help us see ourselves and the world from a different point of view, and impact our leadership, problem-solving abilities and partnerships. Imagine what the world will look like if we all learn to see beyond our narrow-minded or preconceived notions. Siloed thinking diminishes our capacity to connect in a meaningful and impactful way; it's like seeing a movie with one eye or seeing the tree but missing the woods.

As I said before, the key is not only asking questions, but then listening to the answers. It's being open to understanding other realities, understanding cause and effect, and that we can all be a part of making change. It's being flexible, adaptable and resilient.

If we all made a point of doing this, where would that lead us as a global community? I'd say that collectively we would be better able to find the necessary solutions facing our companies and our world.

In this chapter we learned the basic human assets that we all share, and the opportunities that day-to-day life offers each of us to bring out our humanity in its fullest. I also touched on the positive impact that such humanity has on us, others, businesses and the world.

2

What liberates our human assets?

In the introduction, I explained my definition of being human. I expressed how it's not only how we come together as people, but also how we behave for more human interactions to be possible. I explained the importance of self-awareness, and understanding interconnectedness and interdependence, and then in Chapter 1, I highlighted several key human assets that are imperative for better interpersonal relationships.

Now that we understand what human assets are, and their importance in our everyday lives, let's talk about the enablers that either unlock these human behaviours and skills or are only possible when human assets are present. We'll also talk about the attitudes we need to allow all of this power to come to fruition.

Please note that in this chapter I will continue to provide stories rooted in daily interactions, rather than providing corporate examples, as I see human assets and their enablers to be the building blocks to being a more effective leader. In Section 2 I will start to bring my thinking to life through examples rooted in business.

The power of disrupting zones of comfort

We have all experienced that feeling of fear mixed with a pinch of excitement, but when was the last time you felt that way?

I remember the first time I lived abroad on my own. I had just finished high school in Canada and did the typical 'gap year'. I got a job at a hotel in Oxford, UK, and the plan was to get some work experience, make some money and gain some independence. Even though the environment was somewhat familiar, it was safe, and everyone spoke the same language; this was a big deal for me. I was away from home for the first time, completely on my own, meeting new people, learning the norms of hotel working and having to fend for myself.

This might not resonate with some of you, or it may sound silly, but I'll never forget the first time I had to take the bus on my own to the centre of town to buy toiletries. I had of course taken the bus on my own loads growing up, but this felt very different – I was genuinely terrified. I had grown up in a relatively small and safe community, so venturing off like this was a big deal for me. I felt so vulnerable as nothing was familiar to me; I was completely out of my element. As a result, I ended up accidentally leaving everything I bought on a bench somewhere in town.

I remember thinking it was a trip wasted at the time, but on reflection later, I realized just how important that bus trip was; it was a turning point. From that moment on, I started to gain more confidence, push myself further and developed a new appreciation of what was possible. I also became more comfortable with feeling uncomfortable. A few months later, I was travelling Europe and Africa on my own with the money I made at the hotel. This was impossible to comprehend months earlier.

Looking back, I've realized that it's the moments when I've been far outside of my element and challenged that I've discovered my potential or have grown in ways that were previously unimaginable. Having the courage to move outside of our little safe world ignites our sense of vulnerability and evolves our concept of possibility. Stretching to be more than we are makes us feel free and alive, daring and adventurous, and when we do that, it empowers us to bring change to our lives and to those around us.

But as we get older, it's hard to find opportunities that ignite that fire in our bellies. The busier we are, the harder it is to step away from the safety of what we know. We feel little sense of risk when we are comfortable and life feels good. However, existing within that content space can be limiting and doesn't offer much incentive for us to be the best we can be.

> 'My comfort zone is like a little bubble around me, and I've pushed it in different directions and made it bigger and bigger until these objectives that seemed totally crazy eventually fall within the realm of the possible.'
>
> Alex Honnold[1]

By staying in our comfort zones, we're unable to grow and progress, which then makes improvement, achievement and success so much more difficult to attain. When we choose to stay 'safe' from critics, exposure and risk, we essentially give up our right and power to be and do our best, plateauing, and in the end, compromising our progress in life and work. Who wants to live in that way?

Once we get into the habit of looking for opportunities in our daily lives that push us in new ways, it's important to then take that into our professional lives, which we will talk more about in Section 2. Nothing squeezes the best out of us than newness, uncertainty and fear. Embracing challenges develops the courage to take calculated risks, the resiliency to fail and the humility to pick ourselves up and try again. This is what it looks like when your human assets start to come alive, and they are vital skills for any leader that wants to move themselves and their company forward.

The power of wonder

'Do interesting things and interesting things will happen to you.'

Sir John Hegarty[2]

To move yourself and your company forward also requires an active mind, and Sir John Hegarty is a firm believer in the importance of prioritising curiosity to create great innovative cultures. John is the Creative Founder of the global ad agency Bartle Bogle Hegarty (known as BBH) and Co-founder and Creative Director at The Garage Soho & The Business of Creativity. He is creator of the legendary ad campaigns for Levi's, LEGO, Audi, Johnny Walker's Keep Walking and the Lynx Effect, amongst many others, and is also one of TIE's incredible mentors.

His mantra, 'Do interesting things and interesting things will happen to you', is something I personally find so inspiring, and his thinking inspires us all on how to live our best lives by finding inspiration in the day to day. One of the things that John talks about is the importance of 'expanding your personal circle'. John says that it's so important to spend time with people in professions and backgrounds that are different from our own. When we start to talk to people about what they do with a sense of wonder, and truly listen to the answers, it opens new ways of thinking.

Also, different cultural and socioeconomic backgrounds – be they race, nationality, language and/or upbringing – allow for new perspectives and viewpoints. If we're only talking to people from the same situation or background as us, it's unlikely we're going to think in diverse ways. Talking to different people enables us to empathize, be more culturally intelligent and see things in novel ways.

One of the challenges of getting older and more specialized is that our bandwidth narrows, the path gets more focused and we can lose our sense of wonder. When we are younger, we have lots of firsts: first time skiing, first time playing carnival (a big thing here in Brazil), first time taking the bus, first job, first car. But as we get older, our responsibilities increase, and we simply become more restrained. Success can become defined by a good job, a nice house, an expensive car and fancy holidays, and we become less interested in the exciting opportunities that get us thinking differently.

'Be constantly curious to be constantly inspired.'

Sir John Hegarty[3]

That said, I think it's safe to say that in our hearts most of us yearn for more. With a strong sense of wonder we expand our awareness, awe and appreciation of things that are different from what may be expected. The lives we have created for ourselves may have become restrictive, and breaking out of routines can be hard, but it's important to keep pushing for those firsts, and find new ways to enrich our lives by talking to people we wouldn't normally and shaking up the way we see ourselves and the world.

Leaders with a sense of wonder create opportunities to better understand others and develop new perspectives that lead to the development of assets such as cultural intelligence (CQ). This is about creating the right circumstances to challenge calcified assumptions and the space for creativity and innovation. This is what is needed to foster the groundwork for more adaptive and innovative organizations.

The power of constraints

'Push through boundaries to unlock potential.'

Sir John Hegarty[4]

The ability for people to innovate also increases with a healthy dose of constraints. Constraints are a wonderful way to show people what they are capable of, and what individuals learn when times get tough is often what makes them stronger. 'Necessity is the mother of invention' is a popular and widely used phrase, illustrating how constraints, the limitations that impact one's ability to do something, can be sources of opportunity. But how can an obstacle become the way forward, and how can the restriction of certain conditions increase creativity and innovation?

Experiences that excite us and force us to find a solution to a challenge unlock the potential in an obstacle. When feeling connected to a task, and truly motivated by it, it's easier to see an obstacle as an opportunity. Therefore, to turn it into something encouraging, people must see it as a stimulus for positive change and an opportunity to explore something new.

The same is true when looking to find a solution to a challenge. Rather than looking at the resources available (time, money, people, ideas), and seeing them as limited, people need to find value in the opportunity, accept it and build on it;

it's about being resourceful. How can the people in our networks help? What can be traded for support? How can something be repackaged to create new value?

Similarly, there is power in adversity. When people transcend adversity, abilities are often unlocked that people never even knew were there. Setbacks and obstacles also help condition individuals to deal with future challenges because the more they are faced with, the more resilience is developed. Like the children on the boat that I talked about earlier, a life at sea, which is never smooth as the saying goes, helps make anyone more resilient.

I love the growth analogy linked to lobsters and constraints. They are interesting animals, and the way they grow is a great way to think about growth in general. Lobsters are squishy animals that live in rigid shells, but the shells don't expand. As they grow, the shell starts to feel confining, and as they start to feel uncomfortable and under pressure, they realize they need to shed their shells. As a result, they go under a rock, cast off the shell, and then grow another one; and this keeps happening. The stimulus for a lobster to be able to grow is the need to feel uncomfortable.

Our lives as humans are clearly much more complex than that of a lobster and its shell. We also don't have the privilege of knowing, as lobsters do, when our comfort zone turns to be a trap, hindering our growth to reach our full human potential. Sara Tate uses another great analogy in her book *The Rebuilders*.[5] She talks of the comfort of a nice bath that we sit in while it gets slowly cold without us noticing. Our zone of comfort can leave us stuck in positions and places that don't really suit us or serve us anymore (relationships, roles, jobs, etc); and it's not even noticing when the bath is stone cold.

The key with the lobster and with the bath is to be on the lookout for when we are stuck, not moving forward and not growing, and be ready to shed our comfort zone to reach our destiny; to see times of stress as signals for growth and to use adversity properly by growing through it.

'You gain strength, courage and confidence by every experience in which you really stop to look fear in the face. You are able to say to yourself, "I have lived through this horror. I can take the next thing that comes along." You must do the thing you think you cannot do.'

Eleanor Roosevelt[6]

When I spoke with Sara Tate recently she talked about how the more we encounter setbacks, the better we get at encountering them.[7] She also said that discomfort isn't just a stimulus for growth, but also for strength. There was a wonderful example that Sara told me of how the natural world brings this to life. She talked about environmental researchers that created the Biosphere 2 project in the US, which is the largest closed ecological system ever made.[8] Their mission is to serve as a centre for research, outreach, teaching and lifelong learning about Earth and its living systems, and through their research they found that trees grew faster inside than outside the biosphere dome.

Initially, faster growing trees were seen to be a huge breakthrough. However, the results weren't as positive as they first thought. They discovered that a sheltered environment led to weaker trees; to mature, they had to go through the natural stages that all trees need to go through, and they needed to feel that stress. It turned out that the lack of wind meant that the trees didn't develop 'stress wood', which is what is needed for strong growth. The analogy is perfect: without this component the trees simply couldn't support themselves in the long run. The trees needed stress to survive.

I spoke with Michael Jager, Creative Director of Solidarity of Unbridled Labour, about this.[9] In response, he referenced a quote by Alejandro Jodorowsky: 'Birds born in a cage think flying is an illness.'[10] He said that it's a brilliant insight from Alejandro, as it so appropriately speaks to thought and action-limiting frameworks many people trap themselves in, almost seeing that freedom of expression and thought as an illness. He said that the moment you start to open your mind, stretch your head and unlock that feeling of perspective and possibility, it's then that you start to develop your key human assets.

But it's also important to remember that once people do push the envelope, things may not always go as planned, and that's fine too. One of the most reliable indicators of true leadership is the ability to take a challenging event and learn from it. The skills needed to transcend adversity and emerge stronger and more determined than ever are the same ones that make for extraordinary leaders.[11]

This is not about being reactive, defensive and dramatic in difficult moments. It's about being responsive, curious and focusing on growth and learning. It's remembering that when times get hard, in life and work, it's then that you find a part of you that may not be seen very often. Resilience is all in the mindset. Things can always get worse, and things can always get better, and at the end of the day, it's up to us to choose the outcome.

The power of perseverance with passion

There are two words in the Brazilian language that for me help sum up the Brazilian people and their method to accomplish positive outcomes. In English, the words 'jeitinho' and 'gambiarra' translate to 'the little way' and 'a creative solution to something'. These are sometimes seen as a negative, but I think the positive connotations far outweigh the undesirable.

These two words articulate the Brazilian people's incredible ability to always find a solution to something. No matter the resources available – be it money, time or people – there is always a way to make something possible. This is the jeitinho. It may be hanging off the back of the bus while it hurtles along a major road to avoid paying a bus ticket; and yes, that would probably be considered the negative connection to the word. But the ability to innovate and find solutions to everyday challenges is in the Brazilian blood, and this ingenuity finds its way into almost everything that most Brazilians put their hands to.

A gambiarra takes this a little further. This is still being innovative and looking to find a solution to something, but the gambiarra is the actual creation of an improvised solution to resolve a problem. If someone is short of money, it may be creating a line of electricity from the main source to their house, which means they don't pay an electricity bill. Again, that would probably fall into the negative connotation category. But when it comes to fixing things at home that break or getting stuck in the sand with a car, leave it to the Brazilians to find a solution. They have an incredible ability to not give up, but to also come up with a creative improvisation that will get the job done.

To bring the power of jeitinho and gambiarra to life, let me tell you a story about a boat sailing from Cape Town to Rio de Janeiro in 2020. This is about how a toilet managed to get unblocked and an Italian coffee maker saving the day. Warning: you may not ever see your morning coffee the same way again after reading this.

My partner Guga is a professional skipper. Just before the pandemic, he sailed, for the third time, the Cape2Rio regatta. It's a sailing race that has been running between Africa and South America since 1971 and runs from Cape Town to Rio de Janeiro. In the middle of the Atlantic, one of the toilets broke and it needed to be fixed. But when you're at sea, the rules are different to when you are on land. Regularly you are pushed to your limits and many times the only person that can find the answers is you; 'no' just isn't an option.

While sailing in windy and wavy conditions, Guga and the owner of the boat were inside the hull dismantling everything to figure out what happened (I mean, I personally couldn't think of anything more horrible). However, in the middle of the autopsy, a vital piece of the toilet equipment fell into the sea.

A total disaster. Or was it?

Guga then remembered the Italian coffee maker that was in the kitchen. There is a round metal bit on it, and he was certain that piece could replace the bit that plunged to the bottom of the ocean. With metal cutters they removed the piece from the coffee maker, tried it – *voilà*, it worked. The coffee maker was sacrificed, but at least there was a toilet working for the rest of the regatta for the now happy 10 sailors. Until today, if I'm not mistaken, that piece from the coffee maker still keeps that toilet working!

I think we can all learn a thing or two from Brazilian creativity and ingenuity. Constraints are a powerful force and it's incredible to see what people are capable of when they must do something. So, it's not surprising that when someone regularly has access to big budgets and solutions, it's harder to be inventive. Living surrounded by abundance creates a sense of comfort that neutralizes creative and inventive power. But most of the people who have grown up in Brazil have grown up with significantly limited resources, as is the case in any other low-income market. The result is a group of people who are notorious for finding a way to accomplish something creatively and resourcefully.

But when people do have options, and aren't forced to respond in constrained situations, it's much easier to give up. If someone doesn't *need* to do something, it's often hard to stick with it; unless another ingredient is present – passion. When someone really wants something, they are much less likely to give up. This is another very important enabler, and when it's present people have a much greater chance of achieving their goals.

In today's ever-changing business environment, success hinges on the capability to adapt and thrive in challenging situations. But the ability to be creative and find innovative solutions to difficult problems requires attitudes of perseverance and grit. To not give up and have that mental toughness to persist with a challenge, even in the face of real adversity, is only possible with passion, and that only happens when people feel connected to something meaningful, motivated by it and bought in. This is the burning desire which is untouched by upbringing, obligations or duties. The human assets outlined in Chapter 1 enable such connections, and this is why leaders need to understand their importance. The combination of human assets with attitudes of perseverance and grit makes the attainment of any difficult objective possible, and any leader that gets this alchemy right becomes unstoppable in the process.

The power of a positive mindset

> 'If you change the way you look at things,
> the things you look at change.'
>
> Wayne Dyer[12]

Unstoppable people are also determined by how they behave and respond to things. Thoughts drive our emotions and our behaviour, and as a result, our reality is created by the way we think; how we think really does matter.

When I was eight, a group of teenagers decided to grab me when I was walking home from school and put a switch blade to my neck. They did it simply to frighten a small kid, which of course worked. I was traumatized after that. But what was shocking wasn't how I reacted to the situation; I would have happily had my parents walk me to and from school every single day for the rest of my life. What was incredible was how my parents dealt with it, and I'm pretty sure it's made me who I am today. 'Don't let the meanies win.' That was always my Dad's attitude, and as a result, shortly after the incident I was walking to school on my own again.

When September 11th, 2001, happened, I was in the air flying from the UK to Toronto. The airspace closed while we were mid-flight, and I have never been a relaxed flyer. The conversations on board were far from relaxing, and I ended up being impacted by that incident as well. When I was worried about flying again, my Dad told me that 'we can't let the meanies win. You need to keep going.' Even when he was diagnosed with a brain tumour and was receiving treatment, he named the cancer 'the meanies', and the treatment was blasting them. 'All meanies are bullies and cowards at heart, and fear, negativity and acceptance fuels them,' he told us.

My Dad wasn't into being a victim; instead, he chose to be positive, resilient and always move forward. He helped us understand the muscle of self-empowerment, and the capacity we have within ourselves to make change and to face possibilities when there seem to be none. This mindset is so important today.

There's a world view called wabi sabi, which is rooted in traditional Japanese aesthetics.[13] (Not to be confused with wasabi!) It's about choosing to accept imperfection and seeing beauty in asymmetry, simplicity and things that are rustic and incomplete. Over time, wabi sabi has evolved to a Japanese ideal of being light-hearted and hopeful. It is about seeing the best in things that aren't perfect, a 'wisdom in natural simplicity' and 'flawed beauty'. It's a liberation from a material world and an acceptance of a simpler life. It's finding the most basic and natural objects interesting, fascinating and beautiful.

Brazil has a similar concept: 'caprichar'. It's a verb, and it says so much about many Brazilian attitudes to life. The definition when you translate to English is 'to perfect something', but that definition doesn't do it justice. The true definition suggests more is not better, you can do so much with so little, and beauty is in the appreciation of care and detail put into something. It is, again, a choice about the lenses used or the perspective taken when looking at something without judgement.

I walked into a restaurant recently and all I could think about was how creative the interior design was, even though it was clearly not expensive. There were straw lamp shades over numerous warm light bulbs hanging from the ceiling, creating beautiful shadows on the wall. The wooden tables were simple with Portuguese ceramic tiles covering the tabletop. Plants hung from the ceiling and covered the walls and other surfaces. It was gorgeous, simple, warm and beautifully put together.

Brazil is full of people 'caprichando' in the way they dress by wrapping a scarf in their hair to add extra flair, or even how they set up a table for a birthday party in the way they place the food, choose the type of food or even the colour of the food, carefully considering how the colours work together. To 'caprichar' is more than just design or being creative; it's about seeing beauty in the little things and stepping out of conventions. It's not getting hung up on how much money is available or the resources that someone has at their fingertips, but instead, it's an attitude. One of not being a victim and instead embracing what you have and making it beautiful; and such a capacity to turn the negative into a positive is simply awe-inspiring.

When things go wrong it's so easy to fall into a downward spiral, especially when everything happens at once. It can feel as though the world is against us, and we've all been there; it's far from an enjoyable place to be. But our internal perspectives create mental models that then mould our interaction with the world. If we make a conscious effort to change gears, even when nothing that is happening is under our control, things often start to evolve. This is the power of a positive perspective – and the ability to see the good in any circumstance. More often than not, by thinking more positively, solutions start to appear and the negative energy begins to change.

I once saw an interview with the Dalai Lama on how to deal with negative emotions and not fall into the victim mentality trap.[14] In the conversation he explained that negative emotions are related to two things: the first is a self-centred attitude, and the second is accepting life as it seems. His advice is simple; it's to realize that 'nothing exists as it appears.' He also says that negative emotions are based on appearances. If we realize that nothing exists as it appears and have the wisdom to not internalize what is happening, making it all about us, we can transform those negative emotions.

> 'It is not events that disturb people,
> it is their judgements concerning them.'
>
> *Epictetus*[15]

Our feelings are valid and the impulses that come in the face of those feelings are as well, but the action we take is optional. To be more in control of our actions, we need to start tuning into our inner radio, which is our unconscious mind. It's important to pay attention to our thoughts and make them conscious. When that happens, we are better able to have control over the outcome of our reality.

Positive thinking starts with encouraging a positive mindset. When people have a positive attitude, they are not only better able to find solutions to problems, innovate and overcome obstacles, but positive thinking also reduces stress levels. When someone is less stressed, they are calmer, think more clearly, simply nicer to be around and better able to manage others.

Leaders that can maintain a more positive attitude towards work create an environment where employees feel motivated, engaged and empowered. A culture of optimism and enthusiasm is created, one where people are encouraged to embrace challenges with an optimistic outlook. This supportive and inclusive work environment fosters more collaboration, creativity and productivity, and demonstrates how a positive mindset can unlock more potential in a company.

The power of lived experience

'There is no such thing as neutral education. Education either functions as an instrument to bring about conformity or freedom.'

Paulo Freire[16]

There are a few ways to unlock new ideas and learn something new. Think about how children learn science when they are around 10 years old. They digest the information in a couple of ways; either by reading a textbook and trying to understand the theory or by watching the teacher carry out the practical experiment. The first method inevitably results in memorizing abstract definitions, for example, about dilution, concentration and the point of saturation. But the information only becomes clear the moment the teacher pulls out a glass, some water, a spoon and sugar. Through the simple experience of putting the sugar in the water, it's much easier for children to see and understand these concepts. People may learn new information or techniques, but until they apply that thinking through actions, consciousness remains unchanged.

Theoretical and academic learning is the acquisition of knowledge and tools through literature and theories. Experiential learning turns this knowledge into wisdom through the act of doing. We need both. It's when reality hits that people realize they have the necessary tools and start to understand how to put them into practice. Also, information alone doesn't make someone more empathetic, courageous, more culturally intelligent or collaborative. I'm not sure it's possible to teach resilience in a classroom; however, experiential learning can do that in spades.

September 2021 marked the 100th anniversary of Paulo Freire, the patron of Brazilian education. He was a visionary because of a simple but powerful conviction: the role of education should be to create more conscious students. His method was to educate in a way that inserted the lessons into the students' day-to-day lives, as opposed to traditional learning methodology, which he called 'bank education'. This was where teachers held the knowledge and simply deposited that onto the students.[17]

I also believe that the role of education should help people discover and develop their innate potential and talents; this is the power of learning. But we must remember, education does not transform the world. Education changes people, and then people transform the world. We need to find ways to connect with people so that education is truly transformative.

For that to be possible education needs to be oriented to meaning and purpose in a changing world, rather than mere content delivery for students, and I believe that experiential learning is the most powerful way to unlock that meaning. There is a reason why my friend Rick Wheatley, Founder of the advisory firm Systems7, uses experiences that combine natural immersion and adventure sports as a tool to develop people. His work helps professionals break out of the old ways of thinking to see new possibilities that enhance commercial success, while creating the future we need. In a conversation we had about growth and development, Rick talked about the importance of developing self-awareness and how that can be done with experiential learning.[18] He does this through various learning activities but finds special power in situations where people abandon the familiar, including sailing and climbing mountains. He talked about how he takes people to the edge of their mental map and nudges them off, saying that these experiential opportunities immerse people in a situation that overwhelms their system, which then causes an evolution.

In July 2023 my partner Guga was in a European sailing regatta. He and the other sailor on board, Zé, were on the return leg from Horta/Azores to Sables d'Olonne/France, going 19 knots in the early evening, and suddenly they heard a *huge* bang and felt an impact. They were 150 nautical miles from shore, it was getting dark, and water started pouring into the bow of the boat. This was when things got hard. The first pump to remove the water suddenly stopped working, and once they got the second pump connected (which wasn't easy nor straightforward), the motor, used to run the pump, stopped working. Water was up to their knees, batteries were covered with water, and they started to prepare the boat to abandon it.

But even in the face of significant adversity, they kept going, drawing on their knowledge and the limited resources they still had at their disposal. It was the middle of the night at this point, waves over four metres, and water still coming into the boat. They shut down all the electronics, were plunged into complete darkness, and no longer had access to their GPS or other important technical equipment. But this allowed them to use the batteries to run the pump, and after rerouting the boat to Spain, made it to shore 22 hours after impact.

It doesn't necessarily take hitting a whale at full speed in a sailboat off the coast of Spain to find that part of you which you don't see very often, but experiential learning is indispensable for developing leaders. It provides people with the opportunities to plunge into situations that force them to see themselves and their surroundings differently, while expecting them to respond on their own terms, cultivate self-awareness, adaptability, problem-solving skills, an ability to collaborate and discover their resilience. It's the secret to unlocking people's potential and is a transformative approach that bridges the gap between theory and practice.

Lived experiences that excite and engage us push us in new ways and create situations where we can be in reflective contact with our own thoughts, feelings and desires. We learn more about ourselves, creating a more realistic self-image, and therefore a better ability to regulate ourselves and respond to challenges. We develop the human assets of courage, perseverance and optimism, which in turn help us to deal with the ever more complex environment around us.[19]

In times of significant change, such as the type of global and social transition faced today, it's more important than ever for leaders to develop their inner capacity so they are able deal with these increasingly complex challenges. When people experience uncomfortable situations, they are forced to find the person inside of them that can rise to the challenge and find the solutions they wouldn't normally be forced to find.

Opportunities that allow people to practise leading in real circumstances, face challenges head on, make decisions on their own terms and learn from feedback are key to unlocking human assets and developing effective leaders. I'll go into this in more detail in Section 2.

The power of a beginner's mind

'If you feel safe in the area you're working in, you're not working in the right area. Always go a little further into the water than you feel you're capable of being in. Go a little bit out of your depth. And when you don't feel that your feet are quite touching the bottom, you're just about in the right place to do something exciting.'

David Bowie[20]

The first time I understood the power of being immersed in real circumstances was when I finished my business degree through a university exchange to Bangkok, Thailand. This was without question one of the best things to have ever happened to me and was probably one of the catalysts to setting up my business; but not everyone thought I was making the right decision when I signed up for the Thai exchange opportunity.

I was studying business at what is still considered the best business school in Canada. There was a lot of prestige and expense wrapped up in the degree, and as a result, the exchange location was important to many people for reasons that were different to mine. The business programme was famous for shaping future investment bankers and consultants, so many people chose universities in Europe and the UK, and a handful in the bigger centres of Asia such as Hong Kong and

Singapore. But I chose Bangkok, Thailand. I'd never been to Asia before and in my mind, this was an experience of a lifetime. An opportunity to go somewhere new and to be out of my depth. I applied, and to my delight, was accepted. I was the only person from my university to go to Bangkok, and once I arrived, was one of four foreigners at the university. I was in my element.

Nevertheless, I will never forget the conversation that I had with a fellow student before I set off. I remember being stopped in the halls and she asked me why I was leaving the incredible business school to go to a place like Thailand. She said that I was losing out on a world-class education and that it was a big mistake.

To me, the decision seemed so obvious. A textbook or classroom setting would never create that state of not knowing. I wanted to see the world through new eyes and see things as if it was the first time that I was seeing them. I needed to have the different exposure, feel the culture shock and experience the discomfort; only then my eyes would be opened.

David Bowie made a career out of not fully understanding things. He thrived on feeling lost, and he made a point of constantly putting himself in situations that gave him the space to create and learn new things. It was this space that fuelled his reinventions.[21] Zen Buddhism has a concept for this, and it's called the 'beginner's mind'. It's an invitation for all of us to experience life in a way that is unburdened by the past and by previous knowledge. It's about finding ways to empty our mind so that we have the space for new things and chase what is novel to us.

Taking it one step further, let's compare the beginner's mind with the expert's mind. People who are experts often find themselves trapped by their expertise, looking for assurance in ideas and solutions that have worked in the past. Being an expert can sometimes hinder exploratory thinking that is needed to discover radical new ways of doing things, but the beginner's mind loves uncertainty and searches for the space to learn something new. It's being open to the possibility of not knowing, no matter how expert one is.

This way of seeing the world is game changing. It prompts leaders to question and reassess deeply held theories, traditions and conventions, which leads to the disruption of the status quo. It helps them come up with unorthodox ideas, and as a result, drives companies in completely novel directions. In an era of continual intellectual, technological and environmental disruptions to market norms, widely unconventional ideas – plus the perseverance, guts and grit to implement them – can be the difference between survival and obsolescence for companies and the human race. A beginner's mind, no matter how expert we are, allows for the creation of groundbreaking solutions to be possible.

––––––––––

What we learned in this chapter were the various powers that we can use to set free the human assets that shape our everyday lives and that are equally responsible for the impact on leadership, business and the world.

3
The impact of using human assets

In Chapter 1, I explained the human assets that make life and people better and that also provide the building blocks to improve leadership. In Chapter 2, I explained the enablers that unlock these competencies and the attitudes needed to sustain this change. In this chapter, I'm going to explore what happens when people ignite their human assets and the real potential that we all hold to impact the lives of others around us.

What you'll see is that it doesn't matter where a person comes from, the sector they are in, their age, gender or financial status. What unites every story in this chapter is people's ability to tap into their human skills, and the proof of real impact when individuals have a raw desire to challenge the status quo and the right attitude to thrive.

The impact of compassion and agency

During the COVID-19 pandemic we saw people coming together with the sole mission of helping one another. The challenge of a global pandemic liberated people's humanity, and as a result we saw the implementation of so many innovative social solutions and movements.

Living in Brazil I saw, first hand, the impact of a pandemic on a place with limited infrastructure. It was shocking. Through my work I'm also in touch with non-profits and people in 26 other countries around the Global South, and the challenges they also faced were similar. The impact on people's lives from the poorer communities around the world during the pandemic was devastating. Many people from the more vulnerable areas don't have access to basic sanitation or running water, so regular hand washing, or even regular baths, were impossible. Houses and streets remained full of people, so 'social distancing' was not an option. Also, many people who come from the poorer communities rely on informal work to make money, experiencing real poverty. Few have savings, and like many other places around the world, shops remained closed for weeks at a time, tourism halted and there were no people in the streets to spend any money.

People very quickly started to go hungry. I would have numerous people, daily, coming to my house asking for food. When Brazil became the epicentre of the virus, we didn't just hear that people were going to die of coronavirus, we kept hearing that people were going to die of hunger. Many non-profits that my company works with around the world started to spring into action. Their focus may have been art and dance for children, or work with human rights or education, but many of the organizations put aside what they did and focused on getting food into the mouths of the people from their communities. Their main goal was to keep people alive.

One movement stands out in my mind as it changed the dynamic between those helping and those receiving the help. It was started from scratch by a group of friends in the northeast of Brazil who weren't prepared to sit back and watch people starve because of the pandemic, but they didn't want to create a traditional system of handouts. They wanted to construct a mechanism that empowered people from the local area, provided them with a sense of worth, independence and community at a lonely time and enable them to be the drivers of the change that needed to happen.

The solution was a women's kitchen called 'Cozinhas Afetivas' or 'Affective Kitchens' and if you find them on Instagram, they describe themselves as a food security project in Olinda, Brazil.[1] But what is so special about this project is that instead of just handing out food to people in the community from the back of a car (which then isn't valued in the same way, and is often sold for drugs), the women from the community are responsible for making the food and feeding the people from the local area. The relationship immediately changed.

The group of friends created the logistics and conditions for this to be possible. They bought the stoves, pots and pans. They found the space to house the kitchen and put together the group of people to donate regularly. Then the women from the community prepared the food and ran the project.

To give handouts of food that is ready to eat is important in situations of emergencies, but in the long term, a system like this isn't good as it's demoralizing, isn't empowering and it creates an unhealthy dependency on others. People need to feel responsible for their lives, and this project stands out because it solved a real problem while respecting the dignity of the people through compassion and activating human agency for the good of everyone in the local area.

The same dynamics also work in leadership and business. Compassion creates stronger connections between leaders and their teams, which then helps facilitate collaboration, builds trust and leads to more empowered employees. By better understanding the people who work with them, what their needs are and what makes them tick, leaders can harness worker passion and energy to create mutual benefits for everyone. I'll go into more detail about this and provide concrete examples of successful companies that are doing this well in Section 2.

The impact of empathy

Dijalma is a known psychiatrist from the northeast of Brazil, and he is recognized in his local community for truly understanding the basic needs of the people there. Psychiatric help in Brazil is difficult. Unless you can afford private care, access to regular support and prescriptions to buy medication isn't easy. If you go into the community where Dijalma currently lives, pretty much anyone on the street will know who you are talking about. This isn't because he is rich, nor because he has one of the best clinics in the whole of Brazil. It's because he recognizes the suffering that the people in his community face and has made it his mission to fight against the system and attend a human need that the system hasn't managed to fill. People come from far and wide to see him.

Dijalma is 82, but during COVID-19 he didn't close his doors. People still came to his house every day, would sit at his dining room table, and he would talk to families worried about their children's psychiatric disorders. He would treat people and give them prescriptions for medication.

I recently heard a story about Dijalma that brought his humanity to life even further. Many years ago, he was working in a psychiatric hospital. One evening the region experienced torrential rains, which created significant flooding in the local area due to bad drainage. This flooding is known to make transport extremely difficult, and things only tend to return to normal once the heavy rains stop or the water naturally drains away.

On this day, due to the flooding, the transport delivering the food to the hospital stopped until the rains subsided, and as a result, the hospital couldn't give the patients and staff their regular dinner. That night a huge riot kicked off inside the hospital because the patients weren't eating what they normally ate and were angry. They started to destroy everything and threw food everywhere. The staff became really concerned.

Dijalma didn't skip a beat. He told the rest of the staff members that he personally would go into the eating area and talk to the people directly, but he needed to be alone. He asked them to keep the door open so he could escape, if necessary, but he said it was important he talked to them all personally. He went in and saw couscous (a traditional Brazilian corn dish from the northeast) strewn everywhere. People were clearly livid.

'This isn't the food we should be eating!'

'This isn't what we eat at this time of the day!'

'We're hungry!'

'We want suitable food!'

'Treat us properly!'

Dijalma simply responded by saying, 'You're right. You are all completely correct. I'd be angry too.' He then went on to explain the floods and that the food had been purchased, but due to everything shutting down and no one being able to get anywhere, the food hadn't arrived. The patients said that no one had told them anything about the flooding or what was going on; they had no idea.

He continued to explain that the couscous was literally the only food that was available and that he would be eating the same thing that evening. He said he would ask for a new batch of couscous to be made for everyone and that he would sit down with them to eat it. Then he went on to say that if the food didn't arrive by the next afternoon, they had his permission to break everything; but for now, they needed to be patient. Everyone cheered, they all ate together, and the food arrived the next day.

The only way that this situation could have been turned around so effectively was through a more human approach. Through the creation of more transparent communication, treating everyone as equals by eating with them and showing vulnerability by going in alone, Dijalma created a feeling of trust. He understood their anger and did all he could to show them he was on their side.

We can bring these learnings into the corporate environment. No matter how difficult a situation is, when we remove ego, show empathy and understanding and demonstrate a deep respect for others, the chances of success increase considerably. These crucial assets create an atmosphere where people feel heard, valued and understood, which then leads to a business environment of trust and understanding, which inevitably facilitates stronger interpersonal relationships.

The impact of self-awareness and living a life with intention

Building interpersonal relationships and influencing outcomes are easier when people have self-awareness. When someone is in touch with their emotions, they are better able to control them and respond to situations in a calm and appropriate way. This story takes things further and illustrates what can happen when someone appreciates the force of self-awareness to specifically facilitate empowerment.

Following the fall of the Saddam regime in Iraq in 2003, the first ever treatment centre for survivors of torture and war violence was opened. The organization is called Jiyan Foundation for Human Rights, and since 2005 they have supported over 100,000 survivors of trauma, terror, domestic violence and human rights violations in the region. As mentioned in Chapter 1, a large part of their mental health work is rooted in developing the self-awareness of their clients.

Asmaa Ibrahim M. Salih, who I also mentioned before, is a psychotherapist and works as the Co-head of the Trauma Care and Health Programme at Jiyan Foundation, as well as an assistant lecturer at the Institute for Psychotherapy and Psychotraumatology at the University of Duhok in the Kurdistan Region of Northern Iraq. During a conversation we had, she talked about the brutal and traumatic invasion of Sinjar, Iraq, by ISIS in 2014.[2] Having grown up in Iraq, and personally experiencing the oppressive culture, the lack of women's rights and the trauma resulting from 100 years of conflict, she knew she needed to do something and has focused her career to support the people from her region.

After graduating with a BA degree in Clinical Psychology she was one of the first people to be hired by Jiyan Foundation when they opened their first in-patient clinic in Iraq, a year after the war. To then provide even better quality of psychotherapy, she completed a three-year Master's degree in Psychotherapy and Psychotraumatology. She told me of her work with the Yazidi women and children in 2015, and she shared stories from the women who personally experienced the horror of the 2014 ISIS invasion. In only a few hours people's lives were destroyed. Women were torn away from their children, many witnessed the murder of their husbands, pregnant women had to escape to the Sinjar Mountains and fend for themselves and their children in the cold, without enough food or water.

When I spoke to Asmaa, I was keen to understand why she got into this work and what was driving her. She was quick to respond. She explained that traumatic events such as these don't just impact the current generation that is experiencing the trauma, but that it is also transferred to other generations. Trauma impacts people in direct and indirect ways and expands out to every aspect of the community through various forms of fear and oppression, stigma and shame. Asmaa ended our conversation by saying that one of the things that most concerns her is that the Kurdistan nationality is lost. She believes that despite the horror they have experienced, the Kurds must not see themselves as victims and that their self-awareness is the key to empowering the nation.

> 'It is the oppressed who makes the oppressor, and not the other way around. We need to work on ourselves, the Kurds, to not feel we are victims.'

> Asmaa Ibrahim M. Salih

As a young person growing up in Iraq, Asmaa experienced significant challenges personally, but also saw people suffering around her. She knew that things needed to change. She talked about feeling connected to the women in Iraq, and as a result, has made it her mission to care for future generations using the powers of psychotherapy, self-awareness and empowerment. By working with the Kurds to better understand themselves, she's helping to build a nation of people who are more fulfilled and better able to live their lives with intention.

If a more self-aware population can create a more stable nation, more self-aware leaders will develop a more stable company. The more that leaders can understand what fulfils them, the easier it is to make decisions and respond in ways that are in line with their values. When leaders can make choices that allow them to lead authentically, and live their lives with intention, they are happier, which makes for happy customers and teams, and more successful companies. I will go into more detail about this in Section 2.

The impact of following your inner compass

Another consequence of having a broad scope of awareness is the motivation to care for and contribute to the welfare of something much larger than oneself. This is what it means to have an 'inner compass'.[3]

What is the consequence of someone following their inner compass?

The South African economy for a long time was based on the gold mining industry. The gold was abundant, but it was deep underground, which made it very difficult to access. It was only economically viable to mine if you had a huge number of cheap labour.

As a result, the Chamber of Mines drafted the Natives Land Act that was passed by the union government in 1913, which restricted indigenous African communities to 13% of the land.[4] Over the following decades pressure for arable land within these communities, coupled with a hut tax that had to be paid in cash, resulted in peasant farmers literally being forced underground to work in the mines. By the 1950s, the Chamber of Mines had secured a reliable flow of cheap labour.

The African National Congress (ANC), South Africa's current ruling party, was formed in 1912 to fight that legislation. It took until 1994, following Nelson Mandela's election as president in a newly democratic South Africa, to start dismantling it. Land restitution and the consequences of the mining industry remain major challenges for the democratic government. The latter had tragic consequences in the form of occupational diseases that mine workers contracted deep underground while mining gold, asbestos and coal.

My Uncle Neil, who I mentioned at the beginning of the book, worked in occupational medicine as a multi-faceted specialist. He was a trained physician, specializing in pulmonology, occupational health and epidemiology. During his career he treated hundreds of patients who were suffering from the devastating consequences of the unsafe conditions underground.[5] And he spent years exposing the disease burden that miners faced, particularly the dual impact of tuberculosis and silicon dust.[6]

To quote from one of his last publications: 'In my view, the South African gold mining associated silicosis and tuberculosis epidemic is without precise parallel in human history, when its extent in terms of duration, intensity and magnitude are all taken into account.'[7]

His research confirmed that approximately one in three gold miners who worked for at least 15 years underground risked permanent disability due to lung disease. He also confirmed that the lung capacity of Black miners was the same as that of White miners, challenging the prevailing racist classifications, and enabling Black miners to claim the same level of compensation that White miners received.[8]

My Aunt recounted her memories of Neil coming home at the end of a long day having completed his ward rounds at the hospital, lectured students at the university and completed his occupational health clinics. He would have a glass of wine, dinner with the family and then go to his light box. He would spend hours checking individual mine workers' X-rays, writing up the findings on each one and identifying those with compensable lung diseases.

Doing this research was imperative to challenging a broken system. His research was prolific, undertaking studies across southern Africa, with a team of colleagues and post-graduate students. These studies were successfully used in major class action cases against both the asbestos and gold mining companies, compensating current and former miners.

Neil made it his life mission to make the gold mines safer for the thousands of southern African miners.[9] In addition to his research, he represented the mine workers' union in negotiations with the mining industry and the Department of Labour to rewrite the mine worker safety and compensation legislation. He was fighting this battle up until six months before he died.

Neil's humanity, humility and quiet dedication contributed in ways that left an indelible impact on others. He had the inspiration and courage to not only know things needed to be done differently but did something about it, serving a nation over and beyond his own circumstances.

The specific circumstances of any situation are, of course, going to be unique. In the case of Neil, his work and activism were so powerful because he was operating in the context of apartheid in South Africa. In this book, I am talking about a world that is working at a different point in history and within the confines of market capitalism. I'm not suggesting a world where we stop being commercially active; however, I think the time, money and expertise of business needs to be slanted towards improving the world and the people in it. This change will come down to our behaviours, which are the consequence of following our inner compass.

When people tap into their inner sense of responsibility and truly understand their commitment to the values they hold and purpose relating to the good of everyone and everything around them, it helps ensure appropriate choices and decisions are made in everything they do. Considering the state of the world, and the drastic changes in business that need to be made, giving people the permission to let their internal compass guide them is more important now than ever before.

The impact of resilience

To be able to guide oneself through a difficult situation doesn't solely depend on that person's technical abilities. Success is more often impacted by the attitudes and behaviours that people have when they respond to those difficult circumstances, which we learned about in Chapter 2.

Imagine waking up in hospital discovering you have not only broken your spine and will never walk again, but then learning that you are also pregnant. When Faustina Urassa was about to start university in Tanzania in the year 2000, this was what she was facing. She had been involved in a horrible car accident, and together with her family, they started their journey figuring out what it meant to be a spinal cord injury victim.

For anyone it's an unfathomable situation to be in, but for people in places like Kilimanjaro, Tanzania, it is even harder. Then when being a woman in a place like Tanzania with a spinal cord injury is thrown into the equation, it takes the challenges to a whole new level.

In a conversation with Faustina, she explained to me that she initially saw this as a death sentence.[10] No one in her family, including her, knew what a spinal cord injury was, let alone what it meant for her life moving forward. There also wasn't clear information on how someone with a spinal cord injury could safely deliver a baby. Would her disability compromise the health of her child? Was it even possible for her to ever be independent again?

The challenges she faced didn't let up. While navigating survival strategies for the future of Faustina and the unborn child, her fiancé left her, concerned for what the future held for them. She had to learn how to independently move from the bed to her wheelchair and she figured out how to deliver a baby by pushing (even though she can't feel her body from the waist down). She even managed to significantly decrease complications during birth by physically defying all the odds of delivering the baby without intervention. Faustina discovered the symptoms to look out for related to health issues linked to spinal cord injury survivors, how to care for her baby on her own and how to crochet so she could make a living (and a good one at that!). She even managed to defy so many of the odds and prove that sex and relationships were still possible as a female spinal cord injury survivor.

This is what resilience, determination, grit and self-acceptance look like. She went from a challenging experience and being a spinal cord injury victim, to a woman who refused to accept the status quo on all fronts. Since then, she has continued to thrive as a result.

Having conquered one of the hardest situations imaginable, Faustina knew she had to create something that would positively impact other people's lives. She started Songambele in 2018, which is a grassroots community-based organization in Kilimanjaro, Tanzania, and she is now helping other people just like her. The organization is formed and run by women with disabilities irrespective of race, culture, religion or social status. The goal is to promote and encourage good health, inclusive education and well-being of women and girls with disabilities in the country. It's also focused on decreasing stigma attached to disability, and improving access to health services, education, employment and social groups, helping to provide the structure for those living with the new reality of a spinal cord injury.

Faustina never had any of this support when this happened to her in the year 2000, and it took a lot of blood, sweat and tears to make it to where she is now. She very easily could have succumbed to the challenges she faced, but by digging deep, drawing on everything she had and staring defeat in the face, she overcame significant adversity. This took courage, optimism, resilience and perseverance, but she also could have just left it at that. Instead, Faustina chose to use the knowledge and her unique experience to put it to the service of others.

Imagine the power of leaders like Faustina in business; leaders who can relate to others, embrace a mission, find the courage and have the resilience to pioneer ahead, even in the face of unrelenting adversity. This also shows that no matter where someone comes from, their age, background or physical strength, anything is possible once they've unlocked their power and have the right mindset. It doesn't matter what position someone holds at a company, the experience they've had or where they came from previously — with the right outlook, anyone can become a role model for others and create solutions that can impact thousands of others.

The impact of expanding perspectives

It's also possible to impact the way thousands of people around a nation read by broadening horizons. Imagine growing up and only reading stories that have absolutely nothing to do with your reality; the way the houses are, how the people look, the customs, food and the traditions. Believe it or not, most children in Africa don't have access to books that tell stories they can relate to. African children, if they have access to books at all, read about culture and life in the West, where most of the books come from. Until I met Deborah, this reality had never even occurred to me, nor what impact this reality can have on an entire continent.

Deborah Ahenkorah is from Ghana and she grew up there. Like other African children, she too was reading about white picket fences, great big green gardens and a western reality that she and her friends simply couldn't relate to from a cultural or reality point of view. But she then found herself in the US where she went to university, and it was only when she stepped out of her reality and into the one that she was reading about in her childhood stories, that it all became clear to her.

> 'Where are the African writers? And why is there such a lack of quality children's books in Africa talking about an African reality?'
>
> Deborah Ahenkorah

She started to dig deeper, and the more she researched, the more she realized just how serious the situation was. She came across a grim statistic about children's literature in Africa in the early 2000s. UNESCO's basic principle, 'full and equal opportunities in education for all', remained unattained in Africa.[11] According to Scholar Arthur Smith, 'at a time that Britain was producing 2,000 children's titles a year, Nigeria barely produced 60.'[12]

Deborah started to wonder what the impact of this reality could be long term. As she continued her research, she discovered that according to UNESCO at the time, 35% of adults in Africa were illiterate, which is equivalent to 2.7 times the entire population of the United Kingdom. Africa is the only continent where more than half of parents are not able to help their children with homework due to illiteracy; just think of the impact that reality has on a nation. Literacy is a crucial step to getting the basic skills needed to cope with the many challenges children, youth and adults will face throughout their lives.

Deborah knew she had to do something about this situation, and once she had discovered such a glaring human issue, there was no going back. So, in 2008 she co-founded the Golden Baobab Prize in Accra, Ghana. The Golden Baobab works to change the reality of illiteracy rates for Africans, and the way they are doing it is by helping to make reading more accessible, more relevant and more exciting for African children. Their mission is to foster a sense of self-worth and national/continental pride among children in Africa by allowing them to read about African realities. They do this by investing in African children's writers and illustrators, and the publication and publicity of their stories. This way the children have exposure to African and western world realities and stories, expanding their perspectives and horizons, and strengthening their national pride. Through their literary award they discover, nurture and celebrate promising writers of African children's literature while addressing the issue of insufficient quality children's books in Africa.

Their dream is to see a world filled with wonder and possibilities, one African children's story at a time, and through their partner publishing house, African Bureau Stories, they have been working towards getting African stories into the hands of African children.

Imagine the power of young African children now reading about their reality and also about other countries around the world? It not only impacts their desire to read and increases literacy rates around the continent, but it also provides the gift of new and different perspectives. Had Deborah not stepped out of her silo and into another perspective, would she have unearthed these insights? Would she have set up the Golden Baobab Prize? Would African children have access to African stories?

Challenging how we see ourselves and the wider world and stepping across these divides isn't just good for us; it also has a ripple effect of change. By stepping out of her usual context, a sense of identity was awakened in Deborah. This new perspective, and the desire to find a solution to an unjust situation, has now turned into an African movement; changing the face of the continent forever.

What we learned in this chapter was the power of a person that has unleashed their human potential and what can happen as a result. The stories collectively illustrated that anyone, anywhere and of any age can create change. It's just a matter of developing the human assets, unleashing them and having the right attitude. Now, imagine having these people in your companies. Imagine the passion of someone like the people outlined in this chapter running a project and leading a team. Imagine the kind of company that this type of human leadership builds.

On to Section 2…

Section 2

Creating more human leaders and companies

Why championing a 'people first' approach to business is the way forward, how it's possible and the companies that are thriving as a result.

4

The problem with old business paradigms

In this chapter, I will question the paradigms that supposedly bring success to a company and show that when companies put people first and are more human centred in all that they do, they are more competitive. Expect strategies on how to attract the right people, therefore building more human cultures and happier, more productive individuals. Throughout the chapter I'll question conventional thinking and provide alternatives through stories and examples rooted in business and leadership.

What if the main goal of business isn't to just make money?

'Every end in history necessarily contains a new beginning.'

Hannah Arendt[1]

Before graduating from my business degree in Canada, I had an experience that shaped my life forever. I remember sitting in one of the university's auditoriums where we were all working on our laptops connected to the internet (via a key card stuck into the side of the computer which was very high tech at the time). The professor was lecturing and around me some of my fellow students were day-trading; you could always see when there was a particularly good trade as the group would suddenly start fist pumping one another or let out quiet celebratory yelps of excitement.

The professor then got everyone's attention by asking loudly:

'What's the main goal of business?'

We all then had to chant:

'TO MAKE MONEY!'

Something didn't feel right with all of this; the chant, the day-trading. Looking around me, I was clearly the minority that felt this way. I thought to myself, *surely maximizing shareholder value isn't the only thing that companies should worry about?*

I started to reflect on what that 'chant' implied in real life. If the company that I work for says that the only thing it should worry about is making money, what does that say about me, who works for them? Also, if my goal is to just worry about making money for that company, what sort of life does that give me? That chant suggests that I can't think about anything else. I can't get distracted with exercise or family or friends, there would be no time to look after the space around me, I would need to sleep as little as possible and eat badly and quickly. I just kept thinking, *what a horrible existence. Is that really what working life is all about?* It made me feel as though going to work equalled being exploited rather than valued for who I am.

As I continued my reflections, I started to question what this says about the role of business in society. Is the role of business truly to exploit everything around it to make as much money as possible?

'Why are we here? I think many people assume, wrongly, that a company exists solely to make money. Money is an important part of a company's existence, if the company is any good. But a result is not a cause. We have to go deeper and find the real reason for our being...'

David Packard of Hewlett Packard[2]

What I later realized is that this traditional model, with this obsessive pursuit of the bottom line, robs us of the most precious asset we have: our humanity.

Profit first, people second is at the core of this outdated approach, and this is where business overlooks human needs. Financial gain is the only objective, rather than being a means to a greater goal. It's all about consuming resources with no consideration of the impact, both within the company, but also outside of it. People are just a means to an end, and they are seen as a commodity. Leaders run the business and people just come along for the ride. They are a cog in a machine that is purely focused on making a ton of money.

A company with this focus will eventually lead to a toxic work environment because people are not finding meaning or fulfilment in what they do. This then results in high turnover, bad customer service, a collapse in public trust and no brand loyalty (because customers aren't feeling a connection with that company).

The other option is for a business to refocus and find another way, where people come first. This is seeing people as part of a greater whole; working towards a common goal and purpose. These are companies that are driven by people's needs, by their values and belief systems. This is about empowering the people and allowing them to move the business forward. The outcome of this approach is very different to the previous one, and the next few chapters will bring this to life with concrete results from some very successful companies.

When companies put people first, individuals are content with where they are and stay. In fact, they are 3.2 times more likely to stay if they work in a more human company.[3] They remain where they are because they feel as though they are doing something worthwhile and are being considered as part of an equation of business success. They are more creative and innovative because they have the space to grow and are empowered to come up with new ideas and solutions that they feel they own and are personally responsible for. There is a sense of trust, openness and hope. Everyone is in it together.

The returns are also far reaching. When employees are happy and believe in the mission of the business they perform better and provide better customer service.[4] By embedding values of trust and creating an intrapreneurial environment, the company becomes more agile and innovative. Communities also benefit from more inclusive outcomes, which include decisions that impact the environment.

Business success depends on two things: decisions and actions of people outside of the business and engagement of people who they employ. If people are rewarded for what they value most in life, it makes them better at what they do, which then serves the brands, the clients and the customers they work with. Consequently, the money follows.

There is a clear link between how companies treat their people and a company's profitability. The organizational performance company Contexis, along with researchers at the University of Cambridge, have evidence demonstrating that companies with cultures rooted in human values are proven to have increased human performance, happier people, increased retention and more revenue. Unlocking the power of humanity within a business leads directly to real gains in business performance.[5]

This approach of putting people first creates a more human company, and it's invaluable for any business. In 2023 I spoke with Micael Johnstone, Chief Strategy Officer at Contexis and he believes that better data is key to unlocking the humanity in business. He says it's the data that gives leaders the confidence to change their organizations because, at the end of the day, to reinvent a company to make it more human is scary and takes courage. When leaders can see that it's proven that they can be more commercially effective by unlocking purpose and joy in their people, it makes the change a no-brainer.

John Rosling is the Chief Executive Officer of Contexis and he explained that their methodology has been adopted by organizations in 43 countries and the evidence is consistent across those companies.

> 'Unlocking the power of humanity within a business leads directly to real gains in business performance.'
>
> *John Rosling*[6]

More human companies generate higher revenue than traditional companies by 32%.[7] They deliver outcomes to market two times faster.[8] And they ultimately outperform the S&P 500 by 211%.[9] But perhaps more importantly, these businesses increase the quality of life and welfare for employees, improve the experience for customers, create a more resilient organization in times of external threats and have less of a negative impact on the planet.

But you can only have more human companies with more human leaders.

Leaders need to be aware of the power of their human assets or they need to be willing and able to liberate those skills. It's also imperative that they recognize the importance of having the right attitudes and behaviours that enable that change to happen. Therefore, in order to build more human companies, corporate leaders need to either recruit people who are already in tune with the power of their humanity or develop the individuals they have working with them already.

> 'When an objective is purely financial, the number is reductive and excludes the story from around the number. It's efficiency at the expense of effectiveness. We need to move from a financialised logic of efficiency to counter balancing that with a narrative based logic of effectiveness, and that begins with putting context back in.'
>
> *Paul Skinner**[10]

More human leaders create the context that Paul mentions above. They have the broadened horizons, the empathy and ability of actively listening to other stakeholders around the business. They also have the courage to push the envelope, think critically and adapt when necessary. Companies committed to putting people

---

* Author of *The Purpose Upgrade: Change your business to save the world, Change the world to save your business.*

first, hiring the right professionals and investing in their talent to be more flexible, resilient and, in the end, more human will be the ones to survive and thrive.

What if hiring good humans is more important than just leaders?

I remember hearing about a hiring process at the communications network WPP that has stuck with me since I heard it. I was on the Eurostar with Jon Steel, who was WPP's Global Planning Director and Director of the WPP Fellowship at the time. We were heading back from a week's training session in France with a group of WPP Fellows.

The Fellowship was a special leadership programme at WPP, which ran from 1995–2018. Jon ran it from 2005 until he retired, and the WPP Fellowship was a client of mine for 10 years until the programme ceased in 2018. I worked very closely with Jon over those years.

The programme was designed to create future leaders for the group. Between eight and ten Fellows were hired each year from a pool of around 2,000 applicants. The Fellows would then complete three 12-month rotations in different WPP operating companies, each representing a different discipline and each on another continent. WPP believed that an effective leader needed to be multi-disciplinary – able to step out of silos and be flexible.[11] They needed to be culturally intelligent and able to move seamlessly between different business cultures. Whether Fellows remained at WPP or went elsewhere, almost all attained senior positions very quickly.

As we were whizzing through the French countryside sipping coffee and eating croissants, Jon then started to explain how the rigorous hiring process worked for the Fellowship. I was fascinated. It was something I didn't know about previously and quickly learned why it was so important on several levels. It was completely in line with my interest in human values and more human companies.

Jon explained how important it was that he hired good people. He wasn't just looking for an intellectual capacity to do the job, but for personality that held humanity at its core. When I asked Jon what that meant, he explained that they needed to be kind, empathetic, respectful and in no way hierarchical in how they conducted relationships. He went on to explain that they needed to be interested and interesting. Good people. Authentic. You'd want to spend eight hours on a plane with them; almost everything came down to that.

I was loving this conversation.

'So, what does the hiring process look like if you need to hire a good human?' I asked.

He explained that the selection process started in a similar way any selection process would. Candidates filled out an application that was around nine pages.

There were essay questions where they wrote about themselves and then also submitted a video. Based on that first stage, if they made it to the next round, they then had an interview with someone from WPP HQ. To complement that interview, they would also speak with a 'former Fellow' from an operating company who at that stage would now be a senior employee hired by WPP, but who had also gone through the Fellowship programme previously.

It was at this point in the process that things got interesting. The moment candidates stepped foot into WPP HQ, the interview began. The candidates of course had prepared for the up-and-coming more formal interviews and were ready for the questions, but Jon was keen to see people's true colours, and it was how candidates treated the other people from start to finish that also interested him; the people they weren't trying to impress.

Jon would always ask the receptionist, Maureen, how they behaved toward her on arrival. While they were sitting in reception waiting for their turn to be interviewed, they would also have an opportunity to interact with one another, and Jon would always ask Maureen how they treated the other individuals. Maureen was one of several people with whom candidates interacted during first- and final-round interviews; they created many and varied opportunities for people to reveal themselves.

Reflecting on some of the more extreme examples, Jon remembered Maureen telling him that one of the male candidates tried to hit on one of the female candidates. Another young woman told someone she'd been on drugs when Jon called for their feedback conversation, and someone else bragged about how they had got away with some pretty questionable behaviour in a previous job. As you might have guessed, none of those people ended up getting the job.

Most, though, were rejected based on the interviewers' perceptions of people's personality, their capacity for work, their creativity, their level of preparation or their fit for the business.

There were various other stages throughout the interview process to learn more about people, as well as help candidates see a more human face to WPP. Recently hired Fellows were on hand to talk about their experiences and answer questions in reception, and they always held a dinner on the first night. Even though the more informal settings didn't look like interviews, the interviewing continued; people might drink too much and get sloppy, revealing themselves to be completely socially inept, or others would come out of their shells, having been unable to do so in other settings. Jon created several opportunities for people to shine; or not, as sometimes was the case.

Jon also saw the hiring process as an important public relations tool for WPP. Every year he had 2,000 people applying for 12 available jobs. That meant every year, 1,988 people didn't get hired. Jon wanted to ensure that the 2,000 people going through the process felt that it was the best selection process they had ever been involved in. For those that didn't get a job, he wanted them to go away from WPP understanding why they weren't hired, learning new things about themselves having gone through the process and leaving with good feelings about the company. To make that possible meant the hiring process needed to have an important human element to it where people were treated well throughout. After each round of interviews Jon would talk with every single person personally to give detailed feedback – positive and negative. If they didn't make it to the next rounds, he would explain why, even if it meant bringing up drug taking, and explaining that perhaps next time not to get stoned for a job interview. Every person that Jon came across was seen as a person and someone of value.

When he was asked by Sir Martin Sorrell to take over the Fellowship in 2005, Martin first asked Jon what he thought of the programme. Jon responded saying that while he was a big fan, he felt it was being 'managed, rather than led.'

'So, lead it then,' Martin responded.

To Jon, there is a big difference between management and leadership, and leadership without humanity is infinitely less effective. The success of the Fellowship was rooted in making it more human and it is a great example of finding the right person for the job, and ensuring people are treated well throughout the hiring process.[12]

Hiring people works both ways and it's not only about employers assessing candidates; employees are rightfully also getting pickier when it comes to where they want to work. I recently had a conversation with Gulshanoy Tolipova-Gourdin, Marketing Director at LEGO Group. She talked openly about the hiring process a couple of years prior to working there, and she said that she had a list of companies that she was willing to work at; the list comprised only companies that treated people well, where the culture was known to be a good one, with values that were in line with hers. She said she wouldn't even consider working for any other company unless it met her carefully considered criteria.

Gulshanoy wasn't just looking for a job. She was looking for a place that resonated with her values. More than checking *what* she could do there, she was looking for *why* she wanted to be a part of the company. In the end, her decision was more of a human choice than a professional one.

When she got the job at LEGO, she said she 'felt privileged to work here.'

Wow. Doesn't every company want to hear that?

What if companies choose to be at the service of their people?

I'm a mum of two young girls and have always felt privileged to run my own company because as a parent I have been able to be flexible and fit my children into the various aspects of my life. Then, as the years passed by, I started to see the inevitable and feel even luckier. I know of so many highly intelligent women from around the globe, some Ivy League and Oxbridge graduates, who are now either not working, and therefore not making their own money, or not in the position they should be due to time off from having children. The result is women with low self-esteem, which isn't great for them, and a huge waste of incredible talent, which is a lost opportunity for companies.

This happens because women decide to have children and they then hit that 'maternal wall', which is the form of gender discrimination that working mothers encounter when they need to start juggling children and a job. Finding this balance often requires parents to work flexible hours, and most of the time, the juggling falls into the lap of the mother, which ends up penalizing them from the point of view of career progression. Other women may even have to take a break from work all together to look after children full time, and that inevitably can set them back on the career ladder.

It's not only such a waste of incredible talent to not think of ways to retain this very keen, highly intelligent and hugely capable pool of people; companies are also missing out. Research shows that firms with more women in senior positions are more profitable.[13] They are also more socially responsible.[14] And they provide safer, higher-quality customer experiences.[15] These are only a few of the many benefits.

Isn't it better (and more competitive) to see people as human beings and then find workarounds knowing the real barriers people face in their daily lives? I know this is possible because the business model of The Carrot Collective is rooted in exactly this thinking. David Webster, Co-founder and CEO of The Carrot Collective, has built a new type of agency that delivers innovative creative services to customers; but the key difference is how they operate – they retooled the agency.[16] They have no offices, and this is by design; there is no bias as to where talent is based. The business is built around three core human-centred disciplines – talent, culture and operations.

When they started The Carrot Collective, David and his co-founders asked: 'What do people want and where do they want to be?'

Then they asked: 'And does this impact how they can do their job?'

He and his team realized that by serving their employees (rather than the other way around), they created happier people working with them. They went against the grain of usual business theory, and instead of putting financials first, made culture their priority; they made it all about employees being the customers of a company and thrived as a result.[17]

Jon Alexander, Co-founder of the New Citizenship Project and co-author of *Citizens*, talks about the importance of people being citizens of organizations and not consumers of jobs.[18,19] He says that today we are living deep inside the Consumer Story, 'a foundational story of humans as inherently self-interested and competitive. This story has shaped not just individual behaviour but organizational design, economic theory, the role of government, morality – all of culture and society.'

But as Jon says, there is another way. 'The headlines of our time are enough to make anyone feel helpless. But when we start to think and act like citizens, not just consumers, everything changes.' A citizen is someone who can and wants to shape the world and society that they are a part of and brings energy and creativity to bear on the world they live in. It's about tapping into the resources of everyone and finding the best outcomes as a society. It's being more than a sum of your parts; it's interdependence, it's about being human and knowing what the right thing to do is.[20]

The corporate status quo needs to change, and by injecting it with more inclusivity, equality and flexibility, companies will ensure their survival.

> 'When we understand ourselves as citizens, we embrace a different story of humanity. When we recognize this, we see that we all have power, and we see tremendous potential for change. To unleash this, what we need to do is understand the stories we are telling ourselves, take deep care with our language, and build from there.'
>
> Jon Alexander and Ariane Conrad[21]

What if business as usual is failing to benefit everyone?

> 'It always seems impossible until it's done.'
>
> Robert H. Goddard[22]

Some of the major crises of our time have been a result of the way business is conducted; new paradigms need to be created with different sets of rules when it comes to viewing success, to hiring employees and leading teams.

I'm imagining a world where companies recognize that the traditional corporate standards are outdated and unequal. I see leaders with an ambition to drive a better future for all stakeholders and a commitment to action, impact and doing the right thing. It's recognizing the crucial role that business plays for the good of society, the environment and the people who work for them, and actively creating a better world where everyone as a result prospers. It's going back to a place of balance.

Balance is important in any sector, and I remember learning about the importance of balance in the medical profession when I joined my father at a presentation he was giving for a Canadian Anesthesiologists' Society (CAS) Patient Safety Committee event. At the time, he was the Head of the Anaesthesia Department for a few Ontario hospitals and was also the acting President of the Patient Safety Committee. We were stepping out of the car and about to head to the conference room when an anaesthetist from one of his teams saw him and walked over. I'm certain the man didn't know that my father was about to speak about patient safety.

To make conversation, the individual started to talk proudly of how many 'on-call' shifts he had done that week, which meant the number of times he was immediately available to see patients when requested, often requiring him to be at the hospital and survive on very little sleep. I could see that my father was not impressed. After the exchange we continued our journey to the presentation room and on the way my Dad explained to me that doctors get paid extra for each 'on-call' shift they do, so if they are doing numerous shifts a week, they are making a lot of extra money. He also went on to say that people tended to pride themselves on an approach of being almost superhuman, believing that they could do anything. These attitudes were creating an extremely dangerous culture at Canadian hospitals as exhausted doctors don't make effective ones, and he told me that this was one of the biggest challenges he was having to battle; it also happened to be the subject of the presentation he was about to give.

My Dad recognized the development of a questionable culture of doctors who were more interested in pursuing money and stroking their egos than being concerned about patient safety. The perverse incentives that had been set up had undesirable consequences and were contributing to the increased potential for adverse events during anaesthesia. He set out to use his area of influence to make hospitals safer and dedicated a huge portion of his life to being a patient advocate.

In 2008 my Dad passed away, but to continue his legacy the CAS created a Patient Safety Award in his name the following year called the Ian White Patient Safety Award, established to recognize the best safety-related abstract submitted at the annual CAS meeting.[23] It's reassuring to know that since 2009, Canadian anaesthetists are continuing to work towards promoting safety initiatives throughout the national hospital system.

I see parallels with this story and what I'm seeing in business today. The traditional corporate system still very much acts without humanity at its core and has in many ways monopolized our understanding of how we think and talk about the private sector and business in general. However, there are new forms of organizations that are around now (B Corps for example) and more effective human ways of behaving in the corporate world that are allowing us to re-imagine the fundamental building blocks of business. This is about creating new business models rooted in humanity that replace old beliefs and benefit all stakeholders. It's also knowing that we all can play a role in challenging outdated and unfair systems.

I'm not suggesting that we turn companies into charities, but business also can't continue to make money at the expense of society and the environment. This is about making companies more profitable and competitive by putting humans back into the business equation. Business as usual simply won't cut it anymore, and in the following chapters I will explain how a company can become more human and make that necessary shift to nurture customers and set up employees for success and happiness; techniques that will fuel the growth of business well into the future. It's making the necessary changes to create a fairer world, with business being at the core of that evolution, and in the next chapter I'll explain in detail how this is possible.

'I will not follow where the path may lead, but I will go where there is no path, and I will leave a trail.'

Muriel Strode[24]

What we learned in this chapter was that the established paradigms that define goals, hiring, management and so much more are no longer working in today's reality. Through various examples I explained that once a more human approach is adopted at a company, putting people at the centre of what they do and what they stand for, it will benefit not only their bottom line but also all internal and external stakeholders.

_5_

How a company becomes more human

In this chapter, I will provide detailed stories and examples explaining how a people first approach in business is possible. Expect techniques, strategies and tools that successful companies are using not only to be more human centred, but to also provide a competitive advantage.

Fostering relationships

I have been living in Brazil now for close to 18 years, which equates to having lived through four presidential elections. Considering the political challenges that the country faces, this has also included one impeachment, a former president going to jail, that same former president being re-elected once he was found not guilty, and so much more in between.

I find the polarization in Brazil scary, and in the lead up to any presidential election you start to see a questionable side of humanity – on both sides of the equation.

On October 30th, 2022, Jair Bolsonaro lost the presidential election after one presidential term and Luiz Inácio Lula da Silva won. It was a tight race and when Lula won, I was personally relieved. I never supported the policies of Bolsonaro, finding him a scary, dangerous and unhinged individual whose values couldn't be more different from my own. However, the fact that Bolsonaro almost won proved there is still a large part of the population that supports his policies.

What I find fascinating and scary in equal measure are the conversations that are had when a group of friends get together that all vote for the same candidate. There are many times when I've been sitting around a table at a bar or at someone's house for lunch and the conversation seems stuck on the same subject. Intelligent people who have all gone to good schools, make a good living and have travelled internationally, but they are married to their way of thinking and that's it. It could be either Bolsonaro haters or Lula haters, but the discourse is the same.

The people who vote for Bolsonaro say the opposition voted for a 'ladrao' (or a 'robber' in English). They say that Lula's supporters are communists, want to turn Brazil into Venezuela and are simply economically stupid for driving the country into the ground. At the same time, there are Lula supporters who believe that anyone who votes for Bolsonaro is evil, stupid, not enlightened, not human or simply not as smart as them. You get the non-stop angry labels and name calling – 'Bolso-Nazi' is a favourite. If you voted for him, you're written off and bunched together as this horrible unit that doesn't deserve to even exist.

Neither side reflects on what the other may be feeling or the reasons for their vote. You rarely see humility, doubt, constructive criticism or a desire for common understanding. This last election was tight – there were a lot of people who voted for each side. Shouldn't we be interested to understand why?

In Simon Anholt's book *The Good Country Equation*, he reflects on this current global phenomenon and talks about how the world has been broken down into two warring tribes.[1] You are for Lula or Bolsonaro. Republican or Democrat. Leave or Remain. A Nationalist or a Globalist. Left or Right.

Everyone can relate to relationships lost, shouting matches at family dinners or cutting people out of their lives, all because of different political beliefs. Is this what the world has come to? Do we have to marry to one way of thinking? Should our identity be based on the party we vote for? Is this even healthy?

I would like to challenge this.

Can we ask more questions? Can we try to understand other people's reality and points of view? Can we empathize more and judge less? It's uncomfortable to have conversations with people who think differently to us, but I urge you to have that conversation. Share that space and build those bridges. It does take courage, but this courage creates change. Let's all try to challenge the comfortable reality that we have created for ourselves because the more we do that, the more humane the world will be. It's about different and diverse people coming together and learning from one another. It's about humanity coming first.

It's also important to bring this thinking into the context of business. Sara Tate talks about psychological safety in her book *The Rebuilders* and in it explains how it's a key ingredient for businesses and teams to be able to improve, innovate and progress.[2] People need to feel free to speak honestly and feel supported enough to come up with new ideas; without that freedom, new innovative solutions and problem solving is less likely to happen.

Knowing this is one thing, but being able to do it and making that something tangible within a company is another. It requires leaders to have the communication skills that go beyond simply hearing words that another person speaks, but to also seek understanding. To have the ability to share the feelings of others, while also being vulnerable. None of this is easy, but by mastering this art, it's possible to unlock new thinking and knowledge.

When I spoke to Sara about this further, she provided such a wonderful example from her own experience.[3] She explained that she struggles sometimes to be assertive and have certain types of open, honest conversations. She went on to say that for there to be psychological safety in a workplace, people need to be able to speak honestly and truthfully. To implement ways to break down those barriers and create safe spaces to talk when she was the CEO of a large London ad agency, she found various tools to help her.

One of the tools was something that Jo Gebbia created, Co-founder of Airbnb. It's a tool that encourages people to speak more openly and share respectfully, which I love. The tool is called 'Elephant, Dead fish and Vomit'. To get people talking, get things off their chest and to create connections, he would hold a company meeting, and in that meeting, ask everyone to talk about something that fits each of these subjects:[4]

o   Elephant – big things that people aren't mentioning.

o   Dead fish – events that have happened that people can't get over.

o   Vomit – getting something off your chest.

Not only is this a great way to get people talking honestly, but it connects people around the company and develops trust, which is equally as important. When you have trust, you can then create an inclusive work environment that transcends all the differences.

My friend Sarah Cohen, a People and Culture Leader in Canada, talks about the importance of connections in the workplace, reflecting on Adam Smith's *The Invisible Hand*.[5] The invisible hand is a metaphor for the unseen forces that move the free market economy, but Sarah's takeaway from his work is different to the conventional one. Having revisited his original writings she explained that he was from a time of warlords and oppression. He was saying that when you do something and it produces a positive reaction from somebody, then you know you're on to something and it's something you can keep doing – the invisible hand. In her mind, his theory didn't start in a place about money, it started in a place of connection.[6] Capitalism seems to have lost the human component along the way.

It's a matter of going back to basics and human connection is what is necessary. We need it on teams where leaders see the importance of understanding what's alive and real for people; taking the time to sit down and hear from them. Equally, companies must realize that people want to work for good businesses, and therefore being aware of how an enterprise makes an individual feel is a major element of being more human.

In a recent conversation with Simon Rogerson, CEO of Octopus Group, a company that has invested about £20 billion into different enterprises over the last 23 years, he told me that Octopus' main goal is to 'scare the life out of complacent businesses' and 'shake up sectors crying out for disruption'.[7] Seeing that many parts of modern life don't work as well as they should, Simon and his fellow co-founders decided to change that and have done so in the areas of health, wealth and our future. Octopus builds companies with the single purpose of making the world a better place to live.

I spoke with Simon because I wanted to understand if it is possible to have a highly profitable business, but still put people first, and why that's important. I looked at him from across the table and he was adamant in his response. He emphatically said that before anything else, people need to work at a company that they would be friends with; doing that generates more loyalty. Simon continued, saying that it's about doing the right thing, even when no one is watching. When that happens it means you have a personality and you stand for something, which means you attract like-minded people. So much of this, he said, comes down to how companies make individuals feel.

'If you would take the company home to your mum, you know you're doing something right.'

Simon Rogerson

This is about belonging and the fundamental role that businesses can play in the world today. Simon explained that people long to be a part of something bigger than themselves. In many places around the world, there has been a collapse in trust of the church, with politicians and the media. In such a busy, ever more fragmented world, belonging is much harder. Businesses can take a longer view and they have the potential to instigate huge change by focusing on developing stronger connections. Many people can relate to the numerous businesses that they connect with daily; there is a real opportunity to mobilize these strengths. To do this, companies need to think of the responsibility they have to customers and to employees. Businesses that only focus on profits and consumerism will lose to others that think about how to create a strong identity that people can identify with and feel part of; a place that meets their needs for affiliation, social cohesion, purpose and meaning.

If you create a workplace culture where people are seen and valued for their humanity, they will then want to work hard for the mission of your company. If something is meaningful to someone, and they feel connected to it, they will be engaged, look after it and work towards its success.

Having a north star that resonates with people

A competitive athlete's ability to become successful in any given sport doesn't come down to them being superhuman; there are other important factors at play for success to be possible. I was a competitive rower for a few years. Luckily for me, the province of Manitoba only had about 12 people rowing of my age, which meant we all made the provincial team. We got to compete in national regattas and to experience the incredible camaraderie that comes from participating in such an amazing sport. I always loved being in the eight, all of us rowing together. The sound of the oars in unison over the river, that *swish* sound, then the oar cutting through the water, taking a stroke at the same time, then the flick of the wrists, seeing the oar come out and glide over the water again. There is something to be said about sharing a similar objective, surrounding ourselves with the right people, staying the course through the tough times and together doing what we can to succeed.

I adored the feeling in a boat, and I think the metaphor, although somewhat cliché, works to an extent in business. The more that a company can clearly articulate their culture and beliefs, the more their people will understand how they fit into the bigger picture. It's therefore easier for them to have their personal purpose connect and align with the company that they are working with. To continue the metaphor, the purpose of a company is a bit like the cox, leading the way and providing the constant clarity of the mission. The last 500 metres of any race is difficult; you're tired, stressed, your legs are burning and you can't quite see straight. But the cox is there, keeping pace and directing the way. There is that fixed point all eight rowers need to guide the boat over the finish line.

If the rowers didn't know what they were aiming for or ended up rowing at different speeds, paces and styles, the result would be a whole lot of crabs being caught, oars being smacked together and no doubt a capsized boat. A company needs to be clear why they are in business and what they are working towards; people require motivation to work where they do, and consumers need a reason to buy products or services. If you ask your people why they work for you, will your staff know why?

The business world is of course more complicated than an eight-person scull. It may not always be possible for everyone to 'row in the same direction' and that direction may not always be a constant. I am a great believer in challenging the status quo and it's important for people to question decisions, not just 'row together' because that's how things have always been done. Things do, and should, evolve over time. Nothing lasts forever.

In Paul Skinner's book *The Purpose Upgrade*, he explains how purpose can be our most adaptive capacity as humans.[8] He talks about how human cognition allows us to think about where we are, where we've been and where we are going; humans can transcend circumstances, and as a result, find more imaginative solutions to problems.[9] However, although one's corporate intention over time will probably need to evolve, we do still need to acknowledge the importance of clear objectives to create a better culture and environment for employees.

In 2022, I was asked to speak at a financial services forum in the UK, and one of the questions they posed to the speakers was around the importance of purpose, specifically considering Larry Fink's open letter to CEOs in 2022.[10] A point was raised that day about the impending UK recession and questioned if companies would continue to consider investing in purpose in tough times. The consensus was that purpose would probably take a back seat when purse strings were tightened. Hearing that question, I couldn't help wondering if the leaders of those companies at the event that day understood what purpose was for; it can't simply be an add on. Companies that see it as another marketing strategy will never get it right.

During these turbulent times companies need clear intention and objectives more than ever. The challenges that we face as humanity are humbling, and it's essential that people within companies understand how they fit into the broader equation of what is going on around them. People want clarity on why they work where they work, and what are they doing it for, and the answers to their questions must be clear for it to all make sense and be meaningful.

'Value will change in the post-covid world. On one level, that's obvious: valuations in global financial markets have imploded, with many suffering their sharpest declines in decades. More fundamentally, the traditional drivers of value have been shaken, new ones will gain prominence, and there's a possibility that the gulf between what markets value and what people value will close.'

Mark Carney[11]

This is also why companies need to walk the talk and be authentic. It's no good having beautiful purpose statements and then not doing anything. The purpose and the why need to align to all departments, and everyone at the company needs to be on board. I love how Michael Jager from Solidarity of Unbridled Labour talks about brands. He refers to them as 'bands', and says that however you break it down, be it enterprises of 50,000 around the world or a start-up with three people in a basement, it's a band of people with an intention and a point of view. It's a living organism.[12]

Michael explains that a brand is a set of experiences that delivers on a promise every day; whether it's words, products, images, ideas or cultural manifestations. But for that promise to be possible, it requires a band of flawed, beautiful and surprising people who are human to deliver it, together creating love and desire.

When you see a company, or 'band', as an organic organism, the relationship becomes very different to that of a machine that is there to simply make money. A company shouldn't be an identity you're defending, nor a machine for capitalism. The best brands (or bands of people) are interested, they're curious and they're great listeners. They have cultures built on trust and ownership, and they have human values.

This is not about engaging people for a company's benefit; it's about how companies can deserve people's engagement. The trick is figuring out how to frame what your company is doing in the world and asking whether you are doing something that is worth commitment. It's about knowing how you create value and why you're unique. Then creating a strong and distinct culture that helps attract and retain the best people.

Creating a happy working climate

I've talked about the importance of companies focusing on culture, connection and purpose to reach corporate objectives, but what can we learn from the Swedish military about happiness and the importance of leaders unlocking it in their people to benefit business?

Erik Fernholm, who has a background in Cognitive Neuroscience and Happiness Research and is Co-founder of the Inner Development Goals (IDGs) and 29k, told me about his work with 350 members of the highest levels of Sweden's defence leadership, and how their happiness directly impacts their ability to defend the country.[13] When working with the Swedish Armed Forces, Erik decided to do an experiment. He split the group he was working with in two and showed half of them a short 60-second video clip of something that put them in a negative emotional state, and the other half he primed with a positive clip so they were in a positive state. Once both groups were in different emotional states, he gave them a complex quantifiable problem to solve. Once finished, he showed everyone the results from both groups.

Erik clarified to me that research proving how someone's emotional state can impact their creativity, problem solving and innovation isn't new research; it's been proven many times before. Existing studies already explain why we get our ideas in the shower, in our bed, falling asleep, after a glass of wine, on holiday, when hanging out with friends, etc. But his research demonstrated and quantified the power of someone's emotional state in real time; when the results of his experiment were counted, he showed the Swedish Armed Forces that 400% more ideas were created in the positively primed group than the negative one. With those results he was then able to ask the leaders what it meant to them when it comes to their leadership and their team's ability to solve serious problems that can impact the security of their nation.

When we bring this example back to business, it shows that when staff are happier and in a more positive inner state, it increases their capacity for innovation, creativity and thinking by 400%, which has a direct impact on business results and contributes to a company's competitive advantage. If we know the power of inner states, then surely it is the responsibility of leaders to focus on cultivating the conditions that foster the development of happiness and fulfilment for the people who work with them.

Creating the space to empower others

The world is full of possibilities if people are given the right emotional circumstances to support them and the appropriate space to grow into. The following example is one that I'm not sure I'll ever forget and illustrates an important point. Ten years ago, on a family holiday when my eldest daughter was three years old, I accidentally locked her and the car keys inside her grandfather's car. It was 30°C outside and she was strapped in her car seat. Smashing the windows wasn't a great plan for so many reasons, but the clock was ticking as inside the car it was getting hotter by the minute.

But what happened next was unbelievable. By coaching her, believing in her and never losing hope, she managed to calmly get her arms out of her straps, lean forward to get the key, which was sitting on the arm rest, not drop it and press the correct button twice until she was able to open the car.

On one of my trips to London for meetings, I asked a number of business leaders what it meant to them for a company to 'be more human', and I got so many answers. But a common response was the importance of giving people space and that ideas and solutions can come from anywhere. I heard that space isn't just good for the employees in question, but it's also a competitive advantage for business. The more we believe in people, listen to them and give them the space and confidence to shine, we not only make people feel great, but we also encourage innovative solution generation, which can only be a good thing. If people are given the space, they will step into it.

> 'Leaders become great not because of their power, but because of their ability to empower others.'
>
> John C. Maxwell[14]

Let's take this thinking even further. Rather than only looking at leadership within a business to contribute to the creation of solutions, consider casting a wider net for idea generation. Think of the power if businesses tapped into the ideas, energy and resources of all stakeholders of a company and empowered employees, customers, shareholders and suppliers to help drive user and customer outcomes. By engaging people throughout the entire ecosystem of a business, it not only provides an opportunity to better understand what is happening under the surface, but the prospects for new solutions to be unearthed will increase significantly.

The international law firm Mishcon de Reya is known for being a challenger brand, and they don't shy away from a challenge. They've taken on the UK government more than once in some very famous cases. They were Princess Diana's divorce attorneys, and they took on Article 50 with Gina Miller, proving that exiting Europe without MPs having a vote as well as proroguing (or closing) Parliament were unlawful. To understand Mishcon's success I spoke with Elliot Moss, Partner and Chief Brand Officer, and Patrick Connolly, the Academy Director.[15] Was their success down to their high-profile cases or was there another secret ingredient?

> 'Leadership is not about forcing your will on others. It's about mastering the art of letting go.'
>
> Phil Jackson[16]

They told me that what makes Mishcon different to their competitors is that the firm is not hierarchical and ideas come from anywhere within the company. If someone has a good idea, it will be supported, and I was told that a handful of Mishcon's new business opportunities have come from some of the more junior people there. They explained that to continue to encourage idea generation and creative thinking, their people must feel listened to, confident to speak up and supported. For them, the working conditions need to inspire trust, creativity, teamwork and agility. In short, the culture at the firm is rooted in human values.

Trusting the strength of difference

> 'If you try to be someone else, you'll become nobody at all. The only great person you have the possibility of becoming is the greatest version of yourself.'
>
> Steven Bartlett[17]

Everyone is driven by the external conditions and stimulus around them. There are also chemicals in the body, cognitive bias and so much more forcing people not to live a consciously designed life. But life doesn't have to be lived by default, and it's so much easier when leaders are in touch with who they really are. However, it's not enough to only know weaknesses and strengths; people need to also be clear on what fulfils them.

There is something to be said about stepping into a different part of oneself that is more deeply rooted than the one initially thought to have been constructed. This happens when someone's strengths are aligned with their sense of fulfilment, and the result is people who can meet the world with more reserves of power and resilience.

Sarah Watson is an Executive Coach based in New York and helps people do just this. She 'calls leaders to their greatness' by removing the gulf between what they think they are supposed to be doing versus what their inner drives are actually leading them to do.

> 'There is nothing more powerful than great people firing on all cylinders, but also nothing more destructive or dangerous than people misfiring.'
>
> Sarah Watson[18]

In a conversation I had with the UK strategist Jim Carroll, he brought the importance of aligning who leaders are with what they do with a story of performance appraisals.[19] He talked about going into his boss' office every year to talk through his appraisal. He would hear what he did well at and then hear about things he needed to work on. Naturally, Jim would skim over the positives (we all tend to do that) and then focus more on the negatives, seeing how he could improve; the next year Jim would go back and hear the exact same things again. Until one day he stopped addressing the negatives and decided to amplify the positives.

> 'I learned that in a successful, well-constructed business, you can be surrounded by people who can do the things that you can't do. Your value is to excel at one or two things.'
>
> Jim Carroll

Jim continued to say that some people don't know what they are great at or if that greatness even fulfils them. But, with some self-reflection work, it's possible for people to discover what the thing is that they can uniquely do; the area where they can most add value and then unearth what truly excites them.

But once that happens, we need to take this thinking a little further. When leaders have discovered their strengths and weaknesses and understand what makes them happy, the next step is for them to use that information to know who to hire and how to combine their weaknesses with the strengths of others. This is when we get into the power of diversity and inclusion, and how appreciating one's strengths, weaknesses and fulfilment can directly impact company metrics.

The late cultural anthropologist Dr Angeles Arrien alludes to this in her book *The Four Fold Way, Walking the Paths of the Warrior, Teacher, Healer and Visionary*.[20] She studied the common ways that indigenous cultures throughout the world support creative expression, health and adaptation to change. She identified four major principles that integrate ancient cultural wisdom into today's life.

As part of a training session for a handful of the leadership development programmes my company offers, we adapted this framework and the leadership styles we use are: The Achiever, The Analyst, The Nurturer and The Visionary. For each of these styles, their motivations differ:

o   The Achiever is motivated by results and getting things done.

o   The Analyst is motivated by 'getting things right' and looking into the details.

o   The Nurturer's motivation comes from people and their relationships and ensuring everyone is okay.

o   The Visionary finds motivation in possibilities of 'what ifs', looking to the future and dreaming big.

When we run these sessions there are usually real 'aha' moments as people start to reflect on how the leadership styles are taken into group interactions. I recently ran a workshop with a group of business school students that used the base of this training as its core objective, and it was fascinating to see how the group realized the importance of having an equal balance of styles when working on team projects. Imagine a group only being made up of achievers, for example? I fall into The Achiever group, and I'd hate to be in a group of people all just like me; it wouldn't be much fun (or effective) at all!

Although every leader brings their own unique charm to any group setting, this framework shows us that a healthy group needs a person who takes charge and makes decisions, another who looks at all angles of a situation, another who is concerned about the well-being of the group, and finally someone who leads the group into the future with new and interesting ideas. What this knowledge shows us is that our strengths, weaknesses and motivations will fall into one of these areas, and greater team health comes from a balance of all four.

Once leaders have improved their self-awareness, they not only know their contribution to teams and how to work better in them, they also know that they need to hire people who can do the things that they can't do or are unable to do as well. Strength is in difference. It's not about being surrounded by people who think like us and who do no more than create an echo chamber. The key to a top performing team lies in having talent that complements each other's strengths, people who come from different backgrounds and approach problems in novel ways.

Creating teams of diverse talent isn't a charitable obligation, it's a competitive advantage. Diverse teams are more resilient, more creative, more innovative and more effective, and it starts with fully understanding ourselves so we can then lead others better.

Celebrating egoless leadership and a shared purpose

There is a trimaran sailboat from the northeast coast of Brazil that brings the power of human leadership to life. The boat is called *Ave Rara*, which means 'Rare Bird' in English, and when it was competing in regattas the skipper was my partner Guga.

What *Ave Rara* and Guga have proven together over the years is that you don't need to be rich, have top-of-the-line electronics, a posh interior cabin or the latest sailing gear to consistently win a 300 nautical mile sailing race. What you need is passionate human leadership, a clear vision and the ability to get your crew to believe in the goal, believe in themselves and share the feeling of raw determination.

Ave Rara is a 36-foot project by Dick Newick, made from wood in the 1980s, and is worth around US$40k. Over the years, *Ave Rara* raced against boats worth US$1 to US$5 million made of carbon with much bigger budgets and Olympic medallists as skippers. People from around the continent would sign up to the Refeno Regatta in the northeast of Brazil just to see if they were able to beat *Ave Rara* and win the 'Fita Azul' or 'Blue Ribbon', the prize for being the first boat to cross the finish line of the race. They tried, but in 2004, 2010, 2011 and 2013 they never managed it. *Ave Rara* in its day won the Fita Azul four times skippered by Guga, and every time, completely against the odds.

The sailing was hard and it was dangerous, and in many ways pushed everyone's limits. But after every race, the crew proved what was possible and because of this passion *Ave Rara* has become a legend on the Island of Fernando de Noronha in Brazil, where the regatta ends. People have tattooed the boat on their bodies, named hotels on the island after *Ave Rara*, and if you ask people locally about either Guga or the boat, their eyes light up. To this day, Guga has never held onto a trophy won at the end of the race; he always gave away the trophies to the people from the local community on the island to thank them for their support.

When talking with Guga to understand the secret to these unbelievable results, he told me the key was believing it was possible and ensuring everyone else felt part of the mission. He and his team believed in the design and concept of the boat, and they believed they could sail well with the budget they had; but I think it was more than that. His generosity and charisma make me think of those egoless leaders who credit their teams with the company's success in an authentic and tangible way. Those leaders who understand their strengths and weaknesses, realize they can't do it all, welcome input from others and care about the opinions of their staff. They show vulnerability, admit when they are wrong and let their team shine, passing on the recognition and fame to others involved in the mission, making them feel valued and transforming them into invaluable members of the team.

Ave Rara became a conquest and Guga led that mission. Over the years, a community and a movement were created of supporters and crew members completely different from the typical sports people you see at regattas. It was difficult sailing, but everyone who joined the crew loved it because the boat and the culture aboard defied conventions, stood for possibility and proved the power of what can happen when you believe and feel a part of something important.

The story of *Ave Rara* illustrates the powerful alchemy when a leader and their team share a common purpose, when there is a strong mission and passionate, egoless human leadership. Together they create a potent combination that creates enthusiasm and excitement and turns them into an intense human energy and drive, attracting talent to a team and inspiring achievement that is often beyond what was previously thought possible. Although the best leaders need to have a clear vision, what makes the difference are leaders that build on and use the capability of their team, welcome input from everyone and celebrate the success of others. But most of all, they are passionate, and they aren't solely motivated by power, money or fame. When this passion is there, it's infectious, and almost anything is possible.

———

What we learned in this chapter is what sets humanity free in any business. It's the importance for companies to demonstrate a willingness and commitment to creating a culture of honesty, openness, trust and happiness, for there to be cohesion between people and departments, and a clear articulation of culture and beliefs.

6

The gold dust hidden in the outside-in perspective

In this chapter, you'll read stories that illustrate how valuable co-creation is only possible when all internal and external stakeholders participate in a process and are integral to ideation, business model design and implementation of business strategies. When this is done well, it ultimately helps companies navigate the future and makes them more competitive.

Placing real people in the driver's seat

'Every now and then a man's mind is stretched by a new idea or sensation, and never shrinks back to its former dimensions.'

Oliver Wendell Holmes Sr[1]

I remember Jon Steel, former Global Planning Director for WPP, telling me that if you want to really understand people or a place, you need to ride the bus. Jake Carpenter, Founder of Burton Snowboards and one of the inventors of the modern-day snowboard, did this religiously; only instead of it being a bus, he would have regular conversations with youngsters on chairlifts or on the face of mountains. Michael Jager, from Solidarity of Unbridled Labour, told me that these conversations drove the engineers at Burton Snowboards.[2] New ideas for bindings, for example, would often come about after a conversation with a 15-year-old on the side of a mountain. Jake understood the conviction of a kid who had worked all summer long to raise US$1,000 to get a new board and a season pass.

That passion, conviction and understanding was so much more insightful than an engineer who may not be able to be on snow or at the mountain.

This is the power of people putting themselves in other real people's shoes. When individuals connect with local stakeholders, they start to understand the secrets they hold to so many undiscovered solutions, and this is priceless for successful leaders. I see the power of this in my work regularly.

> 'Working in partnership with a non-profit on our TIE programme really highlighted to me the importance of collaboration with an organization to problem solve. We all love the "big reveal", when in fact, working with a client throughout is so much more rewarding for both parties. It helps to cut through the assumptions we often make and allows a team to get to the point a lot faster.'
>
> Karen Coleman, MD, Archetype, Australia (Next15)[3]

Jan Levy, MD of the UK company Three Hands, works with, as he calls them, 'lived experts'; these are people who have lived experience of a range of challenging circumstances.[4] Sitting in the space between businesses and non-profits, Three Hands brings the voices of charities and the 'lived experts' they support into businesses to help their clients better understand the reality on the ground for their customers in the UK.

I wanted to speak with Jan as I knew his clients worked with him to help them unearth insights and navigate the world of underserved customers for whom digital solutions might not work. There is often a real disconnect with the digital services that companies need to offer the wider population, and the desire that some customers have when it comes to dealing with humans.

> 'For many of us, these developments make banking intelligent, responsive and accessible. But there are some people for whom these sorts of "advances" simply don't work.'
>
> Jan Levy[5]

When talking with Jan, as he reflected on issues many of his financial services clients face, he questioned if the more technical 'advancements' in the banking sector are truly inclusive. He described a recent project with a savings and investments provider to help them improve the experiences of bereaved customers, or the family members of deceased customers, who are left with the responsibility of dealing with their loved ones' finances. Instead of bringing in 'expert consultants' or secondary research findings, Three Hands assembled a group of 'lived experts' in bereavement; people who'd been through the experience – with all of the associated grief, emotion and uncertainty that it brings – to explain what it was like for them and offer suggestions for improvements to the company's processes. Their insights and ideas had a deep impact at both 'head' and 'heart' level in the business and resulted in some significant changes.

Jan went on to explain that sometimes it's the little snippets you hear from 'lived experts' that can have a profound impact on businesses. On a Zoom call between people who feel digitally excluded and staff from a high street bank, a lady with dementia told him that if she gets lost or confused in her town, her bank is her safe space. The people there know her and will call her husband if she needs help. That's not a banking service; to her, it's so much more than that.

He went on to provide examples of neurodiverse people who need to see someone's face to process information more easily; people who feel digitally excluded because of a lack of capability and confidence or cost; or those with reduced or fluctuating mental capacity because of a disability or early-stage dementia, who want to run their own finances but find technology difficult. Chat bots, apps and artificial intelligence just don't come close to that of a thoughtful human, either in person or on the other end of a phone. To fulfil a role in society that goes beyond transactional services, Jan explains that organizations must be able to master human *and* digital. If they can, the future of banking will be intelligent, responsive and accessible.

Opening channels of curiosity and understanding between different parts of society and business not only develops more competitive companies, but also ensures that business is a part of society by creating that human connection. For Jan and Three Hands, this is only possible through conversations with their 'lived experts', and the results are solutions that end up being good for people, good for business and good for communities.

Victoria Brooks, a UK strategist who specializes in the development of stories that inspire environmental and social impact, is also on the front line of insights work with corporates in London, UK. Core to her work is gender equality and the importance of men understanding the barriers women face in the corporate world to co-create tangible solutions at work.

In 2017, Victoria worked with Bloom UK to create The Booth of Truth, which is a safe place for women (and now men) to anonymously share the truth of their struggles for equality in the workplace.[6] The Booth of Truth came in the form of a blow-up igloo that inside had two chairs, some tables, pens of all different colours, cards to write on and a box with a slot on the top. Victoria explained that inside the igloo you would see loads of provocative questions about the barriers to women's success in the industry; questions such as: 'What happened the last time you asked for a raise?', 'Have you ever hidden a part of yourself at work rather than risk your career progression, and if so, to what end?', and many more. It invited people to write their innermost secrets, things they would never say out loud, or even allow themselves to think, onto these cards.

The truths that have emerged since shocked the communications industry in the UK, lifting the lid on sexual harassment, unequal pay, exclusion from office social outings and being passed over for promotion. The Booth of Truth acted as a powerful vehicle to build true understanding on dozens of topics between men and women. These truths were then harnessed in 2019 when Victoria and her Co-founder, Siobhan Brunwin, launched 'The Exchange', Bloom's cross-industry programme with creative, tech and media companies, inviting senior male leaders to be matched with rising female leaders to co-mentor each other on how to close the gender divide in their workplaces over six months. The simple act of sharing lived experiences honestly with each other in a confidential and action-oriented space has triggered deep change.

What started as an experiment with 46 participants in 2019 has grown to engage over 300 UK leaders in 2022 and has proven to be highly impactful. Measured both quantitatively and qualitatively, in 2020, the male exchange participants demonstrated a 493% increase in clarity on which actions will positively impact the gender divide in their business, while women reported a 257% increase. Anecdotally, The Exchange has triggered hundreds of actions taken within UK companies to close the gender divide, one radically candid conversation at a time.[7]

Why has this worked? The men and women involved all tapped into their vulnerability, compassion and visibility of their blind spots. Their needs and wants as human beings were being integrated and honoured internally, creating a more functional and respectful working climate.

Charlie Dawson, Founder of the Foundation and co-author of *The Customer Copernicus: How to be Customer-Led,* talked to me about how we love our own truths.[8,9] He said that we believe them deeply and that our perceptions of the world are affected by influences that we may not even be aware of.[10] The result is we find ourselves trapped in convention and external forces we can't see. He says that we perceive the world most naturally from where we stand, with us in the centre and with all the things that we're used to around us. This is an inside-out perspective.

What I do with my work, and what Charlie does with his, is to help provide an outside-in perspective. As Charlie explains, there are two perspectives that matter; those of the people being served and helped – the customers – and the perspectives of the people who have done things differently that can provide new ideas and inspiration of innovative ways of doing things. But individuals can't just get these perspectives from articles because they end up viewing the information through the filter of their own lens. They interpret it the way they see it and end up ignoring the information that's inconvenient or doesn't fit. This is completely normal because everyone naturally sees the world from the inside out, which is why it's so important to put the effort in to understand different groups of customers or even employees or colleagues that come from unfamiliar backgrounds. The family norms, cultures and work norms quite probably are going to be very different from our own; and those outlooks are gold dust.

'What is true equally with leadership as with customer experience, you presume everyone sees the world as you see it. What then happens is you start to design products or management solutions based on what you like.'

Charlie Dawson

Experiential learning rooted in opening people's eyes to new realities and unfamiliar parts of the world is fundamental to the work I've been doing with my company over the past two decades. You can't get this information from a consulting article, and it's only by understanding people in a visceral way that you can solve many of the problems we collectively face.

For the last 20 years, my company has developed and offered a series of leadership development programmes for professionals with the objective of developing human competencies by exposing people to real challenges in communities in other parts of the world. The leaders we work with are often quite senior and in their usual roles accustomed to being in control, expected to provide the answers to challenges easily or able to unearth solutions quickly. Our approach takes them out of their comfortable space and forces them to see themselves and the world differently, making it much more difficult for them to approach problems conventionally. As they work through any given task, these leaders often feel stuck until they reach out to people on the ground in the part of the world they are working. Speaking to the locals always opens and clarifies their direction, compared to the noodling and discussing they do inwardly as a team. Inevitably, once individuals get a taste of the power of speaking to local people, it changes how they approach their work in their regular corporate roles moving forward.

'People having different ideas beyond their own world is what makes their world richer, and you're able to give more nuanced advice. At the end of the day, the more nuanced and the more textured the advice, the more valuable it is to the client.'

Elliot Moss, Partner and Chief Brand Officer,
Mishcon De Reya[11]

Another reason why it's important to open our eyes to different realities, step out of the norm and expand our minds is because it stretches our brains. It makes us more relatable, more informed and more valuable to our clients and customers.

Treating the planet as another customer

New perspectives can unearth new business opportunities, as Lauren Smith demonstrated after her time in Mozambique. Lauren, a senior account director at a large advertising agency in New York, was on an experiential leadership programme with my company almost 10 years ago. While still fully employed, she worked in Mozambique for 30 days with a marine conservation organization called the Marine Megafauna Foundation (MMF). Her project objective for the programme was to use her knowledge to create materials to help MMF present themselves to high-net-worth donors.

Everyone at MMF was completely dedicated to and passionate about their work; marine biologists devoted to monitoring and researching megafauna like manta rays and whale sharks, and local community education projects were created to decrease pollution of beaches and water and so much more. The cause matters and impacts every single person on this planet.

At the end of Lauren's experience, we reflected on the leadership programme and her learnings and she asked me: 'How on earth can I go back to the corporate world after having this experience and working with people who have so much passion, purpose and desire to challenge the system and make things better?'

I replied with: 'If everyone left the private sector, how will it change?'

That resonated.

After further reflection, she agreed that she's not copping out by working in the private sector, and that she can use what she's learned about herself and the reality in Mozambique to make a positive impact in other ways, leveraging the financial and human resources she had at her fingertips.

Then she started to think about what this could look like in practice. She wanted to impact the private sector from more of a systemic point of view using the skills she had. She returned to New York inspired, saying that she could start to be the driver of change by being the one to come up with the solutions for her clients, rather than sitting back and waiting for that 'perfect brief'.

When considering the problem of plastic in the ocean she remembered a biodegradable, compostable six-pack ring solution that was developed by an ad agency a few years prior and this got her excited: 'I work for an ad agency. I can be part of something like this. I can create these solutions...This is actually the best opportunity I've ever had.'

Lauren is still at that same New York agency today… 10 years later!

> 'This programme was more of a mindset shift than anything else. It was the catalyst that pushed me to think differently and changed the way I tackle problems. My experience fundamentally changed how I interact with the world.'
>
> *Lauren Smith*

For change within the private sector to take place, it will happen from within. By opening our eyes and seeing the world and ourselves differently, we not only realize that we can be the drivers of this change, but that we have more power than we think.

What we learned in this chapter was the power of bringing the outside in and the possibilities offered when leaders engage with the wider world in the same way they attend to internal and external customers.

7

The human stories behind corporate successes

In this chapter, I bring to life the stories of successful companies that are thriving because they are human centred and put their people first. You will see that the companies that win are reassuringly human and that how they behave is as important as what they do.

Bringing out the best in leaders

> 'Without continual growth and progress, such words as improvement, achievement and success have no meaning.'
>
> Benjamin Franklin[1]

The humanity of Leo Burnett is so evident when you walk into this global advertising agency in London; it's alive, it's tangible and it embraces you in unexpected ways. As an anecdote there are two women who bring this feeling to life.

Freda sits at the front of reception. I have known Freda since I was about 21 years old when I worked at Leo Burnett London, and even though I only return a few times a year, she still knows my name, she asks about my life in Brazil and wants to see updated pictures of my children. I'd love to think I'm a special guest of the company, but I assure you, she makes everyone feel that way; people who walk in for meetings, people who drop off packages and anyone who works there.

Freda isn't alone. There is also Anne. Anne has also been there since I worked at the company over 20 years ago; still wearing her exquisite dresses, helping everyone with their logistical needs, but doing it with love and so much humanity. To not only have people like Freda and Anne work for you, but also hold onto them for so long, takes a certain kind of company; one that has a human culture at its heart.

When the news broke that Leo Burnett London won Agency of the Year in 2023, I was thrilled for everyone; I also saw it as the return for creating such a human business. In fitting with Charlie Rudd's leadership style, the Group CEO for Leo Burnett and Publicis.Poke, he accepted the award by recognizing the entire company for their victory: 'This is a win for every single one of us.'

For almost two decades my company, TIE, has been developing 'people-centred leaders', and through them, contributing to more human corporate cultures. Our first leadership development programme, which was only focused on immersive in-country experiences at the time, was with Leo Burnett London in 2007. We knew that immersing people in 'extreme' circumstances and exposing them to unfamiliar realities that put them and their abilities to the test would be a great way to develop the leaders that companies and the world needs. We started with the individual immersive experience, but over the years our offerings have evolved to also include virtual cohort opportunities, as well as a scaled programme that involves up to 500 people around a business and is executed once a month throughout the year.

Whatever the leadership development experience may be, the objective has always been the same: through experiential learning and working on different projects, with unfamiliar people in foreign countries, on issues that impact all of us, we inspire leaders to discover the best version of themselves, open their minds and help them contribute in a more inspiring way to business success.

Leo Burnett London continues to work with us today to motivate and inspire talent while unlocking potential in their people to be better and stronger. Charlie wants his people to step out of the circuit, find their own route and not get stuck in the hierarchy. He says that the benefit of experiential learning is that it has actual implication and tangible value in the real world rather than being theoretical, which in his mind is less impactful.

One of our first ever Leo Burnett TIE case studies comes to mind when I think of the impact that a leader can have on a business once they have discovered what fulfils them, as well as the capabilities they have to *be* more and *do* more. Alice Hooper was an account director at the agency in 2011, and while fully employed she spent 30 days in the northeast of Brazil on one of our immersive leadership programmes. I can still hear Alice saying, 'I've got that now' when we were sitting on a hill about a five-minute walk from my house in Olinda, Brazil, sipping from a coconut and reflecting on her experience.

The programme had her working with a non-profit organization called Communidade dos Pequenos Profetas (CPP), that, when they started to carry out their mission, cared for children that lived permanently on the street in Recife, Brazil.[2] Her project objective was to use what she knew from the advertising world to help develop a communications campaign to generate awareness in Recife's middle class of the organization's important, non-profit work, with a view to help attract donations. To realize her objective, she needed to interact with the young people, many of whom had no families, were addicted to glue and very often crack cocaine, and frequently tortured. In the worst cases, some of the children who were supported by the organization were even killed by death squads – paid to 'clean up' the streets. It was a tough world to understand and be a part of, but her immersion was also necessary to better comprehend the reality of people from backgrounds so unlike hers.

When we were on that hill, she told me that she noticed something different about the handful of other people she knew from Leo Burnett who had been on the TIE programme previously; she said that there was something special about them when they returned to work. At the time, when she saw them walk into the office, she couldn't quite put her finger on it; but on that hill it suddenly became clear to her because she was feeling the same sensation. She had discovered what fulfils her – and now she was on a mission.

The experience Alice had gained was game changing for both her and her company, Leo Burnett London. Once she returned to London, she joined forces with another woman at the agency and together they created a new purpose-driven division within the global Leo Burnett network called Change. In 2012 they won a lucrative new piece of business shortly after Change launched, as well as acquired numerous awards. Leo Burnett Change Chicago even won the first ever D&AD White Pencil that same year, which is the ultimate accolade for creative work that makes a real difference in the advertising industry, for their Recipeace campaign, which was intended to create a movement that inspired conflicting people to come together over food.[3] Alice would often credit our programme for the inspiration and the drive to make it all happen.

The human experience she lived through unlocked a new level of self-awareness, motivation and skills that made the perceived impossible, possible. At the end of her experience, Alice shared this great quote about ambition:

> 'The basic goal-reaching principle is to understand that you go as far as you can see, and when you get there you will be able to see farther.'

> *Zig Ziglar*

This was about a collective grappling with complexity, a fascination with uncertainty and a deep understanding of other ways of doing things. Alice developed new insights, empathy for a truly difficult reality that other people face and a new-found resilience. Leo Burnett London gained not only the power of a more confident and human leader in Alice, but also business growth. A real win–win.

The key with leadership development is to find ways that move leaders from looking at life through a narrow hole to providing them with a bird's-eye view; a much broader perspective on the world and their individual and communal roles within it. To provide alternative ideas that confront existing procedures so that improvements and new solutions and ways of doing things can be developed, people need to think and see things differently.

But thinking out of the box isn't easy and going against the grain is hard because the standard operating procedure is often deeply ingrained, familiar and comfortable. We also need to take into consideration our conditioned behaviour patterns that have been instilled in us from a very early age. These repetitive actions, many of which rarely serve us, often come down to traditional education, a system that tells us there is a natural hierarchy and only one answer to a problem. It pushes people into specializations and into systems, and we are taught not to question things.

Simon Rogerson, CEO and Co-founder of Octopus Group who I mentioned earlier, brought this to life in a conversation we had.[4] Octopus consider themselves entrepreneurs; stepping away from the established ways of doing things and disrupting sectors to make the world a better place to live is what they stand for. Reflecting on the education system, Simon told me that just like we define a business by its bottom line, we define a school by how many stars children receive. Children get an exam, which is about learning, but not understanding, while completely stepping over application. It's about creating a machine where children learn, regurgitate and then forget; it doesn't set people up to be successful as a person, as a businessperson or as a life partner.

Traditional teaching methods just transfer skills or knowledge from one individual to another, but experiential learning gets leaders personally involved and challenges their thinking. People fully immerse themselves in an experience, which helps it become personally relevant, therefore creating transformation at an individual and corporate level.

The world is changing quickly, and more than ever there is a part for people who refuse to be painted into a corner and a role for education to teach the necessary human skills for corporate leaders. Experiential learning solutions are a way to reach these objectives, and if done well, they can bring out the best in leaders by opening people's minds, challenging calcified conventional thinking, injecting people with the confidence to reshape what they do and how they do things, and bringing groups of people together from around companies in novel ways to support the move to a more human way of behaving.

Being a purpose-driven business: from humans to humans

Shortly after my unforgettable September 11th, 2001, flight from London to Toronto mentioned earlier, I returned to London to find my first 'real' job. The odds weren't great as we were heading into a grim economic moment following the 9/11 attacks, but through various contacts and connections, I was lucky to meet one of the partners of, then, Ideas Unlimited.

The small communications company was based in Battersea, London, and serviced some well-known charities such as Macmillan Cancer Support, British Red Cross and Greenpeace, amongst others. I walked into the colourfully decorated office space and into the main meeting room – all windows. I was nervous as I sat there, aware everyone from the office could see me speaking with one of the Directors. But I was quickly put at ease and was sold when I spoke to him; the work I would be doing was completely aligned to my values.

The point at which I joined the agency was the start of an extraordinary story for the small business. At the time that I worked for them, the agency was run by three Directors: Chris Norman was the Director that I worked with, as he looked after the charity part of the portfolio; the other two Directors looked after the commercial brands such as events, horse shows, property and luxury goods. As the company evolved, the not-for-profit arm of the business grew to about 90% of the business. Chris was always interested in promoting more of a human-to-human approach to business; a connection to humanity and values, not just self-interest and commercial outcomes. At that time, the focus on charity clients seemed like the only way to realize this mission.

But then things started to take an interesting turn; he realized there was a better way.

The charity sector, although important, didn't have enough reach, influence or money to make the necessary impact in the world. Chris felt that change needed to happen with business, and he made it his mission to be a part of affecting the system of the private sector. Ideas Unlimited then became GOOD and he became the sole director.[5]

The work at GOOD evolved considerably. They started working with clients to help create and promote their purpose and help them understand the positive social and environmental impact they can have, while creating value for stakeholders, business bottom line and the wider society. He always felt that communication is the strongest weapon to create change; there are brilliant ideas out there, but unless they are communicated in a clear, concise and compelling way, they just won't do anything. But the role of GOOD is less about traditional ad campaigns and more about overall delivery, doing and behaviours; real impact is at the core of GOOD's ethos.

Their first big job was with Mars, helping them define and understand their environmental positioning. The Mars staff didn't appreciate the importance of having a sustainable supply chain, so GOOD created a travelling photo exhibition with the sole objective to re-engage Mars' internal staff with the supply chain and the corporate sustainability practices. The exhibition illustrated how they source cocoa and sugar, the benefits of the relationships with the farmers and how being sustainable impacts communities.

From then on, everything that Chris did with his clients was focused on helping them connect with the human story, and specifically, making things meaningful; reminding them to consider all stakeholders, not just shareholders. This considers the employees, communities and people who are impacted by products in all ways possible and helps them get to the bottom of the commercial imperative. As Chris explained to me: 'Marketing and sales lack meaning if it doesn't have purpose.'[6] I have been fascinated with the GOOD story and have watched as they have evolved in such an authentic way. Everything they do, every step of the way, remains true to Chris' mission of making a difference by changing the system.

I hadn't seen Chris in years, but in 2023 on a trip to London we met up again. I was keen to understand more about what they were doing, especially in the context of Britain's economic crisis post the pandemic; a recession, a cost-of-living crisis, so much talk of AI, jobs being lost, etc. I wanted to know if his business had been negatively impacted; although I knew it shouldn't be the case, perhaps in this context, purpose had been shelved and with all the cost cutting, his clients had returned to business as usual.

I walked into the bustling, colourful office space in southeast London and saw him sitting in a meeting room. He finished quickly and after a tour around the office, we sat down over a cup of tea. I asked how many people he had working for him and he told me that there were just over 60, but that the agency is growing quickly and there was space for another 20. On our tour, I walked past a handful of breakout rooms, a library with two bright yellow chairs and a group of people happily discussing projects. I said that it was exciting to see such a positive energy. GOOD had never been so busy, and it was clear from our conversation that the need for corporate purpose was greater than ever.

> 'People are now wanting to know two things when they go for interviews. How does the company make money and who are they making that money for? If they don't like the answers, they don't want to have anything to do with working there.'
>
> Chris Norman MBE[7]

Chris explained that huge companies in the financial services sector in the UK are struggling for talent because there is a significant lack of meaning. He gave me an example of a recent conversation he had with an investment firm; he's helping them think through some big questions. For example, how can an investment firm alleviate wealth or social inequality? He agreed that they are hard questions to reflect on, but said that if they don't know the answers, then it's important they start to try and find them. 'It's about creating change, being committed to that change and being authentic. If you can't demonstrate your commitment, you're a fraud,' he said.

As we continued to reflect on the return of being more human and having purpose, Chris confirmed that the return is better relationships; they are better with customers, with employees and with communities.

> 'The world is built on relationships, and that is what more human organizations deliver.'
>
> *Chris Norman MBE*

Authenticity is so important to Chris and always has been. GOOD is a B Corporation, which is a private certification of for-profit companies that demonstrate they are meeting the highest standards of verified social and environmental performance, public transparency and legal accountability to balance profit and purpose; and now he's taken things even further by also being employee owned.[8] They have a staff council, which is now the backbone of the company, and the council advises the executive and holds the company to account for their behaviour. Chris explained that ideas at the company come from all levels within the business, and he encourages all individuals to bring their whole selves to work.

Talking to Chris you quickly see that things haven't been easy; it's taken a lot of belief and there have been significant struggles to get to where they are now. But as we wrapped up our conversation, he explained his primary learnings from this journey.

He confirmed the importance for everyone to take purpose and meaning seriously, that kindness is the greatest superpower in the world and that people must have humility to understand that they don't have all the answers. People need to be honest, vulnerable and know that it's okay to make the wrong decisions sometimes. Finally, having a vision is important; it helps to keep one going in the right direction.

> 'If you don't catch up, you will soon be irrelevant and then extinct. It will happen to you, so seriously think about how you plan to respond.'
>
> *Chris Norman MBE*

There is another company that I am inspired by that also developed their business model with people at the core. It was founded by a reluctant entrepreneur and a mum of two, now teenage, children.

Sascha Mayer is the Chief Experience Officer and Co-founder of Mamava, a company on a mission to create a healthier society through infrastructure and support for breastfeeding.[9] Sascha's leadership and her business illustrates three things: the power of a real human insight, how product design can change people's lives and what happens when individuals are empowered.

Three months after Sascha had her children, she was back to work. What that meant for her was needing to use a breast pump in a public space when travelling for meetings, which, as it turned out, was not an easy task. The options to use it were few and far between and none of them were ideal. The only place she could find to pump was sitting on top of a toilet, and the logistics (considering most pumps require electricity) were complicated.

The belief at the design studio where she worked, Solidarity of Unbridled Labour which is run by Michael Jager mentioned a few times earlier in the book, was that design can be used to solve real world problems. The leadership team were always open to incubating game changing new ideas and this was one of them. It was clear that a new product design needed to be created for a function that people had been completely ignoring until then, almost as if it had been a secret that women were struggling in this way for so long.

Quickly, in the face of this need, they started to investigate how to make free-standing lactation suites. The solution needed to be easy for employers and facilities staff to install, and easy for mums to access. In 2015, they raised their first very small round of funding, which allowed them to hire their first employees, and they have been growing ever since then.[10] Mamava currently has a yearly revenue of US$30 million with 75 employees and the #1 breast pump company in the world, Medela, partnered with them as it recognized the potential and power of the small business.[11]

This is what happens when we listen to ideas and truly understand the reality of people around us.

Being in business to save the home planet

'What if everyone recognized their own potential? We would be in a completely different world if we then acted upon it.'

Whitney Clapper,
Community Engagement + Impact, Patagonia[12]

A few years ago, I was introduced to Whitney Clapper who is also a firm believer in bringing in more voices from local communities and leads work focused on community impact and partnerships at Patagonia. I was told we were like-minded souls; that person was right.

Occasionally, Whitney and I come together for inspiration sessions, and I decided to record one on my podcast so that others could join us. It was a chance to understand more about the famous Patagonia brand, their purpose, purpose upgrade and future direction. She has worked at the firm for years and has helped drive intersectional campaigns and initiatives focused on the company's reason for being.

As we settled into the conversation, I asked where she was sitting to provide context for our listeners. She explained that she was in the family room of her house, but she went on. She explained that her house sits on the Unceded Territory of the Chumash in Southern California, currently known as Ojai. This set the scene for our conversation.

As a lover of the outdoors, a job with Patagonia was a dream for Whitney. Her first job was with Merrell in 2003, which then became Chaco footwear, and then Chaco footwear became Patagonia footwear. Her role then evolved into a job in the brand department in 2015.

Whitney explained that she joined Patagonia when the company was rethinking how to share stories across its multiple categories and channels. They already had marketers for sport and product, and a long history of elevating the stories from the activists the company supports, but not a dedicated brand and environmental marketing role. Whitney took on this challenge and more recently has taken on a new role on the environmental activism team focused on community engagement and impact.

This is when the conversation got interesting. Whitney started to help us understand where Patagonia's thinking was and where it is now. She first explained how Patagonia is trying to figure out how to work with communities in a regenerative way. It is trying to understand what impact looks like, and what partnerships and relationships look like with non-profits, sports communities or with people who are new to the brand.

She then got serious and started to talk about the evolution of Patagonia's purpose. She explained that their purpose used to be: 'Build the best product, cause no unnecessary harm and use business to inspire and implement solutions to the environmental crisis.' It has now moved on to being: 'We're in business to save the home planet.'

I asked why it evolved. Whitney explained that it was directly related to the urgency of the climate crisis; that the important evolution of the corporate purpose was driven by the owners and across the entire company.

'The science tells us we have less than 10 years
[to prevent irreversible damage from climate change], and
as a result, everyone paused on what they were doing as a

business because everyone needed to reflect on the business norms and routines and really answer how change was going to happen.'

Whitney Clapper

The business started to ask, across the board, if they were really doing everything possible to be in service to the home planet. The question went out to literally everyone around the business, and Whitney openly admits that everyone is still grappling with the questions. But what is clear is that Patagonia is willing to show vulnerability. They are willing to have hard conversations on how they've done things versus where they want to be going in the next 50 years and admit to not having the answers. They are a company willing to take risks and do what is needed to do the right thing. A company willing to empower their staff to help find the right solutions.

As the conversation continued, it was clear how Whitney's job title, Community Engagement + Impact, came to be. It was a direct response to the questions asked by the company. Whitney explained that to find the solutions to the challenges, the answer is collaboration. It's about coming together across communities, silos and sectors, which is why community work has become an important extension of what Patagonia is now doing.

Whitney talked about the importance of acknowledging our privilege and proactively focusing on justice, antiracism and the importance of opening the space for more collective, unified engagement. She talked about what it looks like to centre people and communities in her work, recognizing that by doing that, biodiversity is saved, as is our planet.

We can't do this alone. We need to come together. More heads are better than one; individually we don't have the answers. We need to be humble, bridge divides and be vulnerable. When I then asked Whitney about the importance of being a human company, her answer was so revealing:

'To me a more human company is an organization that has figured out how to collectively work and has found its place within environmental and social movements. It's about bringing in more voices from the communities most impacted by the climate crisis, the frontlines and getting out of the way.'

Whitney Clapper

We need to see more of this honesty from companies, and we need more people like Whitney being empowered to help find the solutions. Honesty, authenticity and empowerment are exactly how we are going to move forward and challenge the system, and this is the power of rooting your business in humanity.

Forging long-lasting relationships over short-term efficiency

When I moved to London in 2001 and opened my bank account, I had my first taste of what customer service looks like when staff are disempowered. Not knowing anything about UK banks I found the first one on the high street and filled in the paperwork. It didn't seem like a huge decision at the time as I was a lowly paid account executive and my relationship with the bank was minimal; even so, my experience was still far from enjoyable. It was virtually impossible to speak to anyone (even then, when people still picked up the phone) and doing anything bank related was difficult.

Around that time, probably due to my constant complaining, someone told me an interesting statistic. They said you are more likely to divorce your spouse than you are to fire your bank. When I heard that, I knew I had to do something; I wasn't going to let that bank get away with treating customers so badly.

Then I discovered first direct, the bank that picks up the phone after one ring.[*] That was their point of difference then, and in today's digital world, it's even more unique now. I still adore them 22 years later, and I'm clearly not alone. In January 2023, first direct was named the #1 company in the UK for delivering such high-quality customer service according to The Institute of Customer Service.[13]

'As the world of business becomes obsessed with technology, it is perfecting the functional experience at the expense of the human experience. Companies are doing this to supposedly be more efficient, but organizations are now full of humans who are not allowed to act in a human way.'

John Sills[†][14]

According to John Sills, Managing Partner of The Foundation, it turns out that the best way for companies to increase their efficiency is to make things better for customers.[15] That means creating a more human experience for people, but things are heading in the wrong direction.

When I spoke to John about his fantastic book *The Human Experience*, he helped me understand why I love first direct so much; especially compared to other banking experiences that have me wasting hours of my life trying to trick the chatbot system to speak to someone. He explained that while chatbots may save companies money in some respects, they are unable to respond to unscripted

---

[*] first direct is a UK bank and writes their name in lowercase letters

[†] John Sills *The Human Experience: How to Make Life Better for Your Customers and Create a More Successful Organization*. Bloomsbury Business (2023).

human moments that require creativity and spontaneity; the moments that build long-lasting relationships. This company clearly figured this out a long time ago as they are accessible, consistent and empower their staff to be proactive (even if it means having a conversation with a customer at 4am UK time).

I was curious how they are so different and continue to be to this day. John talked about the power of ambition and how first direct have always had the ambition to just be brilliant for customers, in every possible way. They have 'Pioneering Amazing Service' written on their wall in the office; it's their north star. He continued to say that as a result, they make customers feel fantastic because of their ambition. A great service is provided, people recommend the bank and customers stick around. The thinking is if being great for customers is your ambition, then great things can happen.

He said first direct also know that when businesses have happy, motivated colleagues, they create great customer experiences. As a result, how first direct treats their employees is an important part of the equation to creating brilliant customer service. John was at first direct's birthday a few years ago, and he told me about the string quartet that played and the Ferris wheel that was outside. Also, they have a concierge desk at the entrance to the company that is for anybody at first direct to use; people can take anything to the desk and it will get sorted for them throughout the day. He also explained that there is no hierarchy, and they were one of the first companies to have a crèche on site. John confirmed that there is an incredible atmosphere at the company; it's a place where people are genuinely happy to be working.

But there are other examples of banks working hard at their customer experience; one as far back as 1848. I'm not sure how many readers will remember 'The Man from the Pru', but for almost two centuries the insurance company Prudential has understood the importance of developing customer relationships, and they did that through a huge team of 'good men' who represented the company well. 'They had to stand out from agents representing other companies.'[16] What set them apart was the human connection and understanding. Prudential is now a part of the financial services company M&G plc and I have been working with a dedicated customer experience team exploring ways to inject more humanity into the system.

As a result, they are in early development of an online community platform attracting members from across society and exploring information with a human-led, co-creative approach. The sole purpose is to create a safe space for people to connect and engage on topics that are important to them and share ideas that inspire positive action.

As mentioned earlier related to the work with Jan Levy and Three Hands, there is a real tension between financial services moving towards more digitalization and the desire that some people have to deal with humans. M&G plc is also trying to bridge that gap through connection, conversation and mutual understanding, recognizing the importance of being more than purely transactional, but rather of being human. The community that they created is one way that they can facilitate those relationships and connections.

Putting humanity at the heart of design

While buildings meet the most basic human needs like shelter and security, architecture can impact the emotional state of any person who interacts with it; it holds the potential to provoke a range of emotions and can set the stage for social interactions and human connections. People are creatures of context, but it's so easy for them to overlook the effect that the physical environment has on health, well-being and even cognition.

In 2023 my daughter needed to switch schools, and like with any important decision, this came with a whole load of research. For a few months her Dad and I traipsed around various schools, trying to make the best decision for her. All the schools we were looking at were on par when it came to the actual teaching and price, but we had other considerations; distance from home, the material they use to teach, the specific teachers, etc.

One thing I hadn't even considered until I walked into the schools was the actual experience once inside from an architectural point of view. Several of the schools were so starkly designed, I couldn't even consider them as options. I'm not an architect, but I know how I feel when I'm in a space.

Here in Brazil, one variable that needs to be considered in any building is the management of the sun. We live close to the equator, and as a result, the sun is strong and the heat at times is unbearable. One school we went to had floor to ceiling windows, and to cut out the blaring sunshine, the windows were broken up with loads of plant boxes with green plants hanging over the sides. This was not only a great sun block solution, but one that introduced the natural environment, providing that important connection to nature. Another school used natural materials like wood for the desks and even the walls, and light cotton curtains to decrease the sun when it's at the angle to stream into the classroom. Then one was a concrete building on a street corner, with black plastic sticky tape over all windows to block the sun and with no green in sight.

I knew immediately which schools were an option.

But it was only when I spoke with Eliot Postma, Partner and Group Leader at Heatherwick Studio, that I understood why.[17,18] The ones I liked put humanity at the heart of the build. Heatherwick Studio and Eliot are all about reconnecting the built environment with human emotion, and he explained why it's important that buildings respond to our emotional needs.

Heatherwick Studio is a design practice in London, UK. Any project that the studio takes on is led by the human experience first. For instance, they have designed a building for a UK cancer charity that increases the use of natural materials and natural light to increase comfort and restore well-being.[19] They have reinvented the famous Red Bus in London.[20] And they have designed Google's first ground-up campus at Bay View in California.[21]

Google's brief to Heatherwick Studio was clear; they wanted sustainability to be central to all aspects of the design, and they wanted a place that would be more collaborative, joyful, fun and would connect people. Humans needed to be in the centre of the design.

The campus workspace was designed on only two levels. The plan was to allow enough space to house up to 3,000 people who would work together on one floor plate, which required rethinking how large office spaces work. The focus of the design was how a large, connected space can still feel human in scale; it would not rely on the traditional layout where there is undemocratic access to daylight, senior people sitting in offices against windows and everyone else doing the work by the core in the dark spot. This was about creating an enormous, connected floor that is broken down into individual tables of various sizes able to accommodate different team needs. The tables sit under a tent-like roof that has slits throughout, creating windows across the entire enclosure, providing a perfectly uniform distribution of daylight across the interior space. The result is that everyone ends up working in the best space that feels their own, under an amazing canopy, enjoying perfect access to natural light. The floor below houses everything else such as gyms, cafés, meeting rooms and kitchens. Again, every part of the building has considered the human experience.

The building is also officially the largest LEED Platinum building on the planet. This means it's one of the most efficient, healthy and cost-saving green buildings that has been built to date.[22] The canopy roofs are draped with 'dragon scale' solar panels that generate enough power to meet around 40% of the energy demands of the campus. The roof allows for the collection of rainwater, which is then recycled through the site, while retention ponds capture storm water. The interior uses healthy materials and the ventilation system uses 100% fresh outside air. The campus also houses the largest geothermal pile system in North America, naturally cooling the space with the support columns of the building foundation. It therefore has no need for truckloads of water and cooling towers, which are typical in air conditioning systems and buildings around the world, estimated to reduce carbon emissions by almost 50% and water used for cooling by 90%.[23]

Heatherwick Studio shows us that when you have a clear corporate purpose rooted in humanity, it not only impacts your bottom line, but also can make a positive mark on the planet. It's about doing things differently, pushing for broader change in the way that people are thinking about the world around us, and making a real impact.

———————

What we have learned in this chapter is that, contrary to what many people believe, building business, systems and policies with people at the core helps companies not only to achieve their financial goals, but more importantly protects the loyalty of all the stakeholders that make the desired return on investment possible.

But this isn't just about the companies nor just the leaders. I believe business can be a force for good and becoming a more competitive business that is also better for the world is simpler than you might think, and more important now than ever before.

The next section will bring to life how leaders with a more human approach at their core will create a more sustainable world...

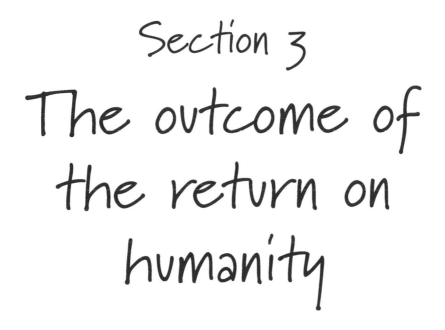

Section 3
The outcome of the return on humanity

When human power is translated into the strategies and actions
that change what 'is' into what 'should be'.

8

Creating the necessary conditions for magic to happen

The purpose of this chapter is to provide evidence of the dividends obtained when leaders make humanity fundamental to the way they conduct their business, impacting not only the bottom line, but more importantly, the world at large. It's a financial and human win–win.

The power of integrating humanity into the financial equation

'Do you know what penguins do in the morning?'

Just before I launched my company TIE in 2006, this was the start of some wonderfully sound advice that I was about to receive from Jeremy Bullmore CBE on one of our regular lunch dates. I was lucky to be put in touch with Jeremy by Sir Chris Powell back in 2005. I had come up with the idea of my company, and Chris knew just the person to help me think my way through the business planning. Jeremy was one of the most widely known and influential thinkers on advertising and brands, whose work at J. Walter Thompson and WPP continues to be used worldwide.[1] His career in the industry lasted almost 70 years.

When I met Jeremy, I was starstruck. I had seen his photo in the *Guardian* newspaper as a regular columnist and in various industry publications. He spoke publicly, authored various books and was an advisor for the biggest communications network in the world. But his credentials and fame weren't what hit me; when I met him, what struck me was Jeremy's humanity. As Jon Steel said in his tribute after Jeremy passed away, 'In an industry of takers, he was a giver.' I was a young account person in advertising when we first met. I had an interesting idea, but not much more; but like so many other lucky people over the years, Jeremy took his time to not only share his wisdom, but to also be a friend. When my father passed away in 2008, Jeremy took my mother out for lunch; when my eldest was born, he made a point of wanting to meet her; and when I would return to London numerous times throughout the year, every year, we would meet for lunch, and he would help me think through so many things related to life and work.

> 'When a penguin wakes up in the morning he waddles to the edge of the iceberg and looks in and he thinks, "Will I have breakfast this morning, or will I be breakfast this morning?" When you launch TIE, you want to have breakfast. You need to get this right.'

Jeremy helped ensure the success of my business through his regular mentorship, and he helped thousands of other people globally equally thrive and be better. He was described as 'Adland's greatest philosopher', and his guidance on corporate culture, work with clients and clear direction on business and leadership was rooted in the importance of implementing a more human approach to business, and it was valued by many corporate leaders.

He was authentic and loving, yet strong and forceful. Empathetic and funny, but also good at setting boundaries. Intelligent and sharp, but he wouldn't want you saying that too loudly; he was incredibly humble. In short, he also had the human qualities that are needed to drive a profitable business today.

At Jeremy's celebration of life in 2023, a passage was read by Rufus Olins from Jeremy's satirical novel *The Quality Quotient*.[2] His book talks about a new metric that reflects on human and corporate behaviour: 'A quotient that ranks companies not on share price or earnings per share or return on capital invested, but on care, compassion and social responsibility.'

I think this passage leaves a lot for us to reflect on:

> '"It's my belief that we judge the financial community too harshly if we think them blind to all but financial considerations. I believe that all decision makers in all walks of life find comfort in the presence of supporting numbers – and that they are right to do so. But is their behaviour conditioned by their exclusive preoccupation with financial data – or could it just be, given the lamentable absence of anything else, that they have no choice? I believe that all of us know in our hearts that the true worth of great companies cannot be determined by return on investment alone. All money is expressed in numbers – but not all numbers are an expression of money. Would you challenge that, Mr Lomax?"

Wisely, Roddy Lomax didn't.

"You yourself, Mr Lomax, described Mr Sandal's management style as magnificent. Absolutely magnificent, I seem to remember. I would agree with you. If more senior businessmen were to follow his example, you believe this country would be a better place to live in. I would agree with you. Your only regret was that 'it didn't count'. And what I am saying to you is this: It can count! That is precisely the effect that a known Quality Quotient will have. Those of us here this evening – we know the worth and the value of social responsibility. Simply apply the Quality Quotient, and the whole world will know it too."'

A reasonable conclusion. The true value of something is not only determined by financial value, but human value also plays an imperative part in this equation; and this human approach to measure success has even expanded to countries. In the 1970s, Bhutan, a small, landlocked kingdom, introduced Gross National Happiness (GNH) as a measure of economic and moral progress, and in 2008 it was formally adopted as a development indicator in their constitution.[3] The objective was to prove to the world that we need to move beyond only a GDP measurement and consider social development.[4]

If we want to assess the true worth of a business, money can't be the only consideration or currency used. As argued in this book, a more human approach to business and life is the new currency for the new world order, which considers the ultimate currency for any human – happiness. Money, fame and power all come secondary to happiness, and although all may be desirable because they can lead to positive emotions, they have no intrinsic value on their own.

We need to be chasing a currency that considers our interdependence, our interconnectedness and our happiness, and the happiness of those around us. That is the return on humanity. When we do that, the rest follows.

The power of forging unlikely partnerships

Although we know we are stronger together, the reality is that we are terribly disconnected as a global community; to contribute to the currency that considers our interdependence and interconnectedness, we need to create environments that facilitate these crucial connections.

There is a lot going on at the moment, isn't there? Economic meltdown. Political turmoil. Alarmingly hot summers. Energy crises. Floods. Droughts. Forest fires. The list goes on – and won't stop anytime soon. It's enough to make anyone feel paralysed or impotent; but I see it as a clarion call for us all to forget about the old ways of thinking and act differently.

Companies can be at the forefront of creating a new world order, and there is a tremendous capacity of enthusiastic and intelligent human resource that businesses can tap into to be drivers of this change; but it won't just happen. The key is creating a conducive environment and the conditions that facilitate transformation and evolution.

The conditions that facilitate this potential are rooted in my definition of humanity, which I outlined in the introduction of the book:

o **Collaboration** (which is linked to interdependence): There is no one person, no one company, no one sector, no one country that has all the answers. We must come together across divides to find solutions. We can't work in a vacuum.

o **Outside-in thinking** (which is linked to interconnectedness): We must dare to branch out, broaden our minds and gain new thoughts and perspectives so we can innovate, understand how all are connected and find the necessary solutions in our companies and our world.

o **Unlocking people's power** (which is linked to self-awareness): When people understand the power that they have at their fingertips, they become unstoppable.

Although it's known that collaboration and new perspectives are crucial for creating sustainable solutions to almost any problem, without outside intervention, it's hard for people to actively seek out opportunities to step out of the normal ways of behaving. For this to be possible, it's imperative to create environments for unique experiences to happen between people who wouldn't usually come together. Finding moments where individuals from different countries, departments, regions and sectors can share something uncommon with one another creates a base for better working relationships moving forward. People build an improved understanding of what others do, find commonalities and create affectionate bonds. New realities are generated that may have been considered impossible previously, and help people appreciate how different variables of a certain phenomenon may fit together.

Through my work over the last two decades, I've seen this power in action. Since 2006 we have been bringing people from the Global North together with others from the Global South, and by joining them we've physically or virtually taken them all to places they never would have expected, linking different worlds and exposing them to previously unfathomable global insights. This exposure not only reminds individuals that we are all interconnected and helps them reflect on the importance of other people's actions to influence their well-being or desired objectives, but it also helps to create unlikely partnerships between groups of people who may not have even known the other existed previously.

In our daily lives we get locked into systems and routines, drawn into technology and get further removed from one another and the wider world. It's hard to snap out of this monotony and we need to consciously break the cycle to open our minds and broaden our networks. This next example brings to life how we unknowingly live disconnected from what is going on in other parts of the world.

Living in the southern hemisphere during the pandemic was a stark reminder of how detached we all are as a global community and how easy it is to only see the world from our own viewpoints. I'll never forget this lesson that COVID-19 taught me, and I was only aware of this perspective because of where I was based. The pandemic of course proved to all of us that something that happens in one place can very quickly impact another and that we all need to come together as a global community to find solutions to a problem. However, the announcements of 'Freedom Day' in the UK when many other countries around the Global South were still in lockdown seemed so strange to me.[5] How could Freedom Day be possible until everyone around the world had access to the vaccine? If a virus is running rampant in one part of the world, and vaccines aren't available to that part of the planet, Freedom Day in the other part of the world simply won't last very long. COVID-19 was a disease of a connected world and burst open the reality that the only way to come to a solution was to come together as a global community.

We can't forget this.

This is a call for all business leaders to focus on creating an environment within their companies that will help their people actively seek out new opinions, different experiences and other ways of seeing the world in order to facilitate the connection of unlikely partnerships to achieve a common goal. As mentioned in the introduction, this book isn't suggesting humanity equals good and business equals bad; it's quite the opposite. What I'm suggesting is that business is one of, if not *the* most powerful forces on Earth to drive change – for good and for bad. It's together we can create amazing things, ideas, aspirations and change in the world. We can do that in business, and it happens when people and companies put humanity into what they do; remember, we rely on one another to find novel solutions and need to be open to other opinions to bring new voices in.

If you want to change the world for the better, the private sector offers you perhaps the most valuable lever to pull, and the most effective change will come about by working together in global cooperation. We not only need to recognize this, but actively create the environment so that worlds can be bridged and exciting new partnerships made.

The power of reintegrating people into society

The prison system and a radio station are a perfect way to illustrate the power of bridging different worlds, and how when that happens, it can impact the rest of society. The conventional thinking is that prison is simply a place for people to suffer by having their liberty removed as punishment for the crimes committed, but it can be a place to reflect, learn, gain skills and be better; if that is the focus, the impact on society can be tremendous, and it's been proven.

In 2023 I spoke with Phil Maguire OBE, founding Chief Executive of the Prison Radio Association (PRA).[6] This is the organization that runs National Prison Radio (NPR), the world's first national radio station for people living in prison.[7] Phil has been running the award-winning charity in the UK since 2006 and has dedicated his professional life to supporting prisoner rehabilitation. The story and the model are fascinating and impactful.

People in prison around the UK religiously tune into NPR. The programmes are created for people living in prison, by people living in prison and only people in prison have access to them. NPR started in 2007 as a single station, Electric Radio Brixton, behind the walls of HMP Brixton London, and now it's broadcasting 24 hours a day, seven days a week, to around 80,000 people around the country. People can expect the usual mix of songs and conversations. There are mindfulness programmes to help ease the stress of daily prison life. They share important information about services, offerings and concerns at the prisons. And there is an important two-way flow of communication between the people running the prisons and those living in them. Without human behaviours, skills and attitudes, what they do would be impossible; it's the empowerment, empathy, listening to understand, connection and trust that makes the organization's work such a success.

When I spoke to Phil, it was clear just how important radio is to this captive audience. Eighty-four per cent of people within the prisons who can listen to the station do so for around nine hours a week. NPR has a direct dialogue with its listeners through messages or letters or voicemails, and the audience informs the development of the station and the content. The people who live in prison are at the heart of what they do; they have given a voice to individuals who wouldn't normally have one and by getting involved with the programme the people who live in prisons develop valuable skills they never had before.

But its significance is extraordinary, not only inside the prisons, but also outside of them. As a result of being involved in an amazing and impactful award-winning radio station, people have gone on to get jobs in the media once they have finished their sentences, providing them with income and a purpose once on the outside; crucial factors that can help decrease re-offending. Also, individuals who have been involved in the project have often then been hired by the NPR when they leave prison; having people involved with the organization who have prison experience is important to them.

The NPR creates a lifeline to people living in prisons. The aim is to reduce re-offending by engaging those who live in prison with skill development, education and discussion, helping them to develop strategies for not only dealing with the issues that led them to imprisonment in the first place, but to also have more of a purpose when they are released.

Treating people who have been incarcerated like humans has not only created a significant level of trust between the people living in prisons and those running them, but it has created a healthier society outside of them. This is how we are all connected; a decision and action made in one place can drastically impact another.

The power of building mutually beneficial relationships

A healthy society comes down to balance; self-interest is not generally civilized and can lead to great inequality and impairment of efficiency. What we need is capitalism tempered by the agency of collective action and a recognition that we are stronger together.

I was in my garden one day looking at the water from the sprinkler hitting the trees above it and what happened next illustrated this thinking for me. Watering the garden at around 4:30pm after a really hot day in Brazil attracts the most incredible wildlife: numerous species of birds appear, including small parrots, as well as the Sagui monkeys. Everyone wanting to cool off, clean themselves and perhaps grab some of the pitanga fruit that hangs off the branches. It's amazing to watch.

Then you start seeing a fight for territory. Certain birds fighting with other birds, monkeys getting dive-bombed by parrots, a cacophony of screeching and a hive of activity. But there is no blood, and it's clear that there is a common understanding in the treetops.

All forms of nature, be it plants or animals, are competitive with one another. They fight amongst themselves, but at the heart of nature is balance and interdependencies between animal and plant populations govern this. Permaculture brings this to life beautifully; the natural order of ecosystems that are sustainable and self-sufficient. A flower needs the bee and vice versa. We need one another to exist and we are more together than we are apart. That or we become extinct.

Bringing this back to the business world, let's consider economics and competitive advantage, which, as Paul Skinner says, was developed entirely by financiers and economists.[8] He reflects on this in his book, *Collaborative Advantage: How Collaboration Beats Competition as a Strategy for Success.*[9] The principal of economics is that you line up the resources you own, manage and control them, and then create superior value for your stakeholders. The problem is that economics doesn't consider the human element to these transactions. Perhaps it should, as Jeremy Bullmore alludes to in his book mentioned at the beginning of this chapter; it's the 'Quality Quotient'.

Business isn't just a deliverer of something of value. As Paul Skinner says, 'It's an enabling mechanism that enables all of its stakeholders to come together and use their agency to improve each other's lives through the nexus of the enterprise.'

When this is understood, the opportunity for success can be lifted substantially. This is about working together, learning from one another and being stronger and more effective as a result.

Related to this there is one memory from my time in Thailand in 2001 that has stuck with me. Outside of my dorm room were several different food vendors; one selling papaya salad, one selling Thai noodles and a whole load selling chickens. Each one was family owned, and it was a family affair each evening; chicken being put in plastic bags by the adults with children playing hide-and-seek nearby, underneath and in front of the food-stall tables. The street vendors obviously made their living from selling their produce and if they didn't sell the food, *their* family had less money for food and school. It was that simple. They needed to make money.

What I found incredible was how they co-existed amongst one another. Not once did I feel as though people were trying to force their produce on me and more than once when I suggested that I liked the look of the other person's chicken or salad, I was encouraged to buy from the other vendor. The western competitive push was non-existent.

Everyone benefits if everyone does well. That has stuck with me for over 20 years.

For centuries, the basic rule of leadership has been competition. The dominant values of leadership have been those of achievement, ambition, power and assertiveness; I win, at all costs. But there is a shift happening. Society is realizing we must move to an age of collaboration and citizenship. An age where the dominant leadership values include caring for others and preserving nature, placing importance on people and relationships, empathy, and emphasizing equality and solidarity. The more human values.

Now that it's clearly and universally proven beneficial to root behaviours and attitudes in humanity rather than competition, collaboration now needs to be the basic rule. This is now an opportunity for our global community to move forward as a group of equals between the Global North and the Global South. This is a chance to shape a better and different world by working together and learning from one another.

To do that we need enlightened leaders who know that global collaboration is the only way we can get there.

———

The objective of this chapter was to illustrate the power people have when choosing to create a better world through more human ideas, approaches and behaviours; it's realizing that an evolution is necessary and then constructing the right environment for change to be possible.

9

The world is a global village, and we are all responsible for its future

In this chapter, I provide detailed stories that illustrate the importance of understanding the reality in other parts of the world and creating connections between sectors to solve the biggest challenges we face today.

Becoming consciously aware that local problems are not isolated issues

'Travel far enough and you meet yourself.'

David Mitchell[1]

In 2012 there was a big problem in Malawi: almost everyone was cooking with open fires. Malawi is a landlocked, least developed country, which means that many people don't have money for electricity and don't have access to gas or solar.[‡] Like everybody around the world, they still need to heat their food, but their reliance on open fires using wood was damaging the environment – and costing lives.

Although wood is a renewable resource, if more wood is burnt than is regrown, more CO_2 ends up in the atmosphere, which is bad for our climate. Not only does this result in greater scarcity of wood, but it also increases soil erosion, river siltation, the sinking of the water table and reduced natural habitat for biodiversity.

[‡] Malawi is a landlocked country in southern Africa bordering Mozambique, Zambia and the United Republic of Tanzania. It is categorized as a least developed country (LDC) and its high dependence on agriculture makes it one of the countries most affected by climate change.

Likewise, cooking with open fires can have significant health implications. Worldwide deaths from lower respiratory tract infections, often exacerbated or caused by indoor air pollution, are estimated to be more than malaria and HIV/AIDs combined.[2] It's believed to be the leading cause of death for children under five and the second leading cause of death for adults in Malawi.[3]

Something needed to be done to promote cooking options that people actually use, are healthier than open fires and require significantly less biomass and other solid fuels. The answer needed to create a scenario of inclusion and sustainability.

That year an organization in Malawi got in touch with us, requesting support from a communications professional. They knew that the answer was affordable and easy to use fuel-efficient clay stoves, but they didn't have the skills to get the word out. They needed to make the stoves 'sexy' to get them into the hands of as many people as possible. If more people used the stoves, it would improve the environment and the livelihoods of the local people of the country, helping to contribute to the sustainable growth of one of the world's poorest and least developed countries.

The ad agency Wieden and Kennedy New York was one of our clients at the time and was involved with our immersive leadership development programme, and Trevor Gilley was the chosen participant in 2012. Trevor worked as a designer at the agency and came from Midwest America. He spent his life creating beautiful ads for famous brands and was very good at it, but his day job didn't allow him to work with strategy or run projects from beginning to end; other people had those roles at the agency. He also hadn't travelled much outside of the US, nor did he have any international development experience.

Trevor spent 30 days in Malawi working with people he had never met before, in a culture he didn't know, to crack a brief he didn't know anything about; but his objective was clear. Most people didn't know that the stoves existed and of their overwhelming benefits, and he needed to unlock demand. After spending time talking about and truly understanding the problems that the organization was facing, the local reality and the best way to get their stoves into the homes of people of Malawi, he and the team on the ground identified two areas that they would focus attention.

They knew that families at home were their primary target users for their stoves, and they needed to transform the stoves into symbols of social status to drive demand on a user level, generating interest in homes by word of mouth.

Their secondary target were large businesses and political officials as they had a vested interest in reducing the pollution and solving the problem of utility shortages. Energy and water outages were a huge issue in Malawi due to the fact they were spending millions on algae prevention at their energy turbines in Lake Malawi. The pollution of the water supply was caused by soil erosion into the lake, triggered by deforestation to supply the increasing demand for firewood as urban populations were booming. To please constituents and existing budgets dedicated to environmental preservation, Trevor and the team knew that this target was a powerful one to support their cause.

By combining these areas of focus and engaging key players (e.g. hotel owners, large businesses, government officials) to back the initiative and place large orders of stoves, the team was convinced it would create a tipping point where the stoves would be readily available for purchase by people who were interested in and attracted by the concept.

The strategy had the everyday person drive the demand, while large investors and influencers would dictate the supply in key locations. The campaign targeted the two main communities that were considered influential to its success.

Without question this experience pushed Trevor's limits, but it also made a real impact. Before Trevor touched down in the country the organization had sold just 500 stoves over two years. Immediately after completing his 30-day programme and launching the campaign, 10,000 stoves were ordered.

But this was only the beginning.

The programme pushed Trevor's creative language and voice to another sector and culture and it had him learning about a different way of life. He only packed with him his talent and creativity and put it at the service of the Malawi people and the reality of their circumstances, leaving behind his role, his culture and any other 'certainty' that could have limited his contribution to the project and team. The development of his human leadership competencies not only influenced a community in Malawi but also made him a better professional back at the agency.

The organization continued to use Trevor's communications strategy and materials after he left, and by 2020 the country reached its own ambitious target of two million cleaner cookstoves.

This was the start of something even bigger.

The original organization we worked with evolved into another organization called the CCC (The Cleaner Cooking Coalition), which is an alliance of people from around the world that play a critical role in driving awareness and advocacy of the need for cleaner cooking solutions, facilitating a just energy transition and working to reach a clean energy future.[4] In 2021, we heard from one of the founders at the CCC; they needed more help.

They had done the numbers and in 2021 there were still 2.8 billion people around the world who didn't have access to cleaner cooking and would continue to rely on traditional stoves and solid fuels to cook over the next 10 years. We were told that electricity wouldn't come close to filling the energy gap and solutions were needed that would work towards sustainable energy transitions for households that are likely to be the last reached in the global transition to modern energy services.[5] The most vulnerable populations are the ultra-poor, those in rural areas with limited market access, and the growing populations of sub-Saharan Africa, South and Southeast Asia and Central America/Caribbean.[6] And the current levels of investment in clean cooking fall far short of the US$10 billion needed to reach universal access.[7]

As citizens of the global village, our individual and collective actions impact other far-away communities; what happens in one place impacts another. To have nearly a third of the world's population relying on polluting open fires and inefficient stoves not only contributes to 3.2 million premature deaths, harms livelihoods and damages the climate and the local environment, but this current situation has a huge impact on our global CO_2 levels.[8]

The CCC team knew what needed to happen; they had to give a voice to the 2.8 billion people and the cleaner cooking movement, and they knew just the place.

In September 2021, there was a UN High-Level Dialogue on Energy, the first one in 40 years. The UN had decided to reconvene this high-level dialogue for energy because they knew the world isn't progressing fast enough on the CO_2 emissions globally. All the big energy players would be there, and Malawi was selected to represent the bottom billions. Their goal was to be 'at the table' in terms of discussions around SDG7 (Sustainable Development Goal 7), which aims to 'ensure access to affordable, reliable, sustainable and modern energy for all'.[9] A global reappraisal was needed on how best to make cooking cleaner, and eventually clean.

What happened next shows the real power of partnerships, and without them, the results would not have been possible. This was a joint effort.

Involved was the local organization CCC, the National Cookstove Steering Committee of Malawi and the Ministry of Energy in Malawi. The team comprised of professionals who have been working on and assessing access to cleaner cooking with the most vulnerable communities across the globe in Malawi, India, Mexico and beyond. Some of the people included Omar Masera of National University of Mexico, a Nobel Peace Prize Laureate on behalf of an Intergovernmental Panel for Climate Change and one of the main people behind the concept of fuel stacking (making parallel use of multiple devices and fuels for different types of cooking practices). Dr Priyadarshini Karve, a guru on household energy in India who has won various prizes for her work on 'intermediate technology' – including the World Technology Award – and is an advocate on meeting people's needs. And Christa Roth, who has worked in Africa on food and fuel systems since the 1990s and is one of the global references on micro-gasification, which will be especially important for the next generation of biomass-based technologies.

This was a hugely experienced team, but they needed help from the private sector to complement the team's enthusiasm, experience and knowledge with professionals skilled in communication strategy, diplomacy and campaigning. This is where my company TIE came in again.

In 2021, we pulled together a virtual cohort of professionals from Switzerland, England and Australia to help the government of Malawi prepare for the high-profile UN energy meeting. We had marketing professionals from the finance sector who were looking for hands on, real-time experiential personal and professional development. A CEO of a London-based impact green fintech called iClima Earth, a company that works to redefine climate change investments, focusing on companies with products and services that can transition the world to a low carbon economy; she wanted to gain insights and knowledge of an area not known by many outside Africa. Involved was also the co-founder of a Venture Capitalist (VC) growth investor (UnaTerra) that is at the crossroad of technology, digitalization, sustainability and social responsibility; he was looking for a deeper dive into the world of international development to better understand the territory.

The result of the short collaborative programme was incredible. Together they created a speech and film that the President of Malawi delivered to the UN meeting, and it was so convincing that it was capable of adding new and crucial champions to help contribute towards the realization of their mission. The team created a cleaner cooking pledge that was later signed by the First Minister of Scotland, Nicola Sturgeon, and Hon Nancy Tembo, Minister of Forestry and Natural Resources of Malawi. The pledge was a commitment to cleaner cooking opportunities and to the people who depend on them. Following this, CCC was able to secure a US$50,000 donation to continue their important work.

Our team also received a letter from Malawi's Permanent Representative to the United Nations in New York, Dr Perks Ligoya, acknowledging TIE's help in preparing the country for the UN high-level dialogue meeting.

But what particularly stands out and helps bring to life the power and importance of these types of collaborations were the personal reflections after the programme.

One of the participants, Luca Zerbini, MD of UnaTerra, explained that even after working in sustainable investments for a very long time, he learned information that he didn't know before. The issue of the 'bottom billions' and the impact of CO_2 emissions from the black carbon emissions produced globally from burning wood to cook was not talked about anywhere.

'Everyone in the investment space talks about solar, wind and electric. They are the solutions that everyone wants to invest in. But it was clear that it doesn't make sense to invest in clean cooking equipment for a group of people that can't afford it. The result are stoves that won't be used and a problem that remains.'

Luca Zerbini[10]

The current global energy solutions aren't considering the reality of people in the poorest areas of the world and applying an advanced western approach leaves billions of people behind.

As Anaïs Nin said, 'We see the world not as it is, but as we are.'

What this programme showed everyone was that once you understand an issue and the real context, you can start to provide something that is affordable, simpler and more adaptable; the solutions need to be the right ones for the reality in question. Once you pull together the right people to solve the real problem, anything is possible, and everyone wins.

Reflecting on Trevor's thoughts after his experience back in 2012, his words still ring so true 11 years later.

> 'The clarity I got from Africa is that we are all part of a global community, and we rely on each other for the sustainability of our environment. There are communities all over the world that could use help from its fellow mankind. We are in an industry that has close relationships to some of the biggest brands in the world. We need to find a way to use these connections and resources to make a positive impact on the world around us. Helping to give exposure to the humanitarian work our clients are already doing is the first step. Beyond that we can find a way to create relationships on both sides of the field. We are a global network, and we must begin forging relationships one email at a time.'
>
> *Trevor Gilley*

This is the return on humanity. All the results mentioned above are what happened when we chose to connect and collaborate to overcome the cultural, language and interest barriers that can separate us from the well-being of other human beings. Imagine if everyone did this. What would the world look like?

Leveraging the power of the private sector

> 'There is a crack, a crack in everything.'
>
> *Leonard Cohen*[11]

This is a story that illustrates the true power of the private sector when it chooses to stand up for the well-being of other humans, understands the importance of putting people first and not only protecting financial transactions.

It was an exciting time when Brazil was awarded the World Cup back in 2007. Imagine, the country that has won the tournament five times, and one of the most passionate footballing nations was about to host the biggest, most exciting tournament in the world; football was coming home. How wonderful… or was it? Living in Brazil, we saw the darker side to hosting an event like this.

Once it was known that Brazil was going to host both the World Cup and the Olympics, the government made a commitment to regeneration. However, a large part of this regeneration involved 'cleaning up' areas around stadiums. It was in the name of supposedly creating safer favelas, which are the Brazilian equivalent of a slum or shanty town, and constructing tourist friendly transport systems, but as many of the stadiums were built in poor areas, the result meant that many of the people living there ended up being forcibly evicted from their homes.[12]

What also played into the hands of the government were the low literacy rates and lack of education and information in the areas they were evicting people. The result was that households were easily 'tricked' into signing away their homes, and by the time they realized they'd been had, there was nothing that could be done. It was devasting to see this unfold. There were stories of elderly people who had been living in their houses for decades losing everything, people's businesses being destroyed before their eyes and large families watching their houses being bulldozed.

Not surprisingly, this news wasn't seen in mainstream media. Only a small group of human rights organizations started to understand what was happening and made it their mission to do something about it. They called themselves the Comitê Popular da Copa (the World Cup People's Committee). The group was made up of non-governmental organizations (NGOs), universities and social forums, led by the international NGO Habitat for Humanity.[13]

This group had a shared mission: to fight for the human and housing rights of poor people in these regeneration areas and to ensure the World Cup didn't create a housing, health and humanitarian crisis for Brazil's poor; but they needed help. They knew what was happening and understood what was wrong, but they needed more people with connections to create a bigger movement.

This is where my company came in, illustrating the power of collaboration. One of our clients mentioned earlier in the book is the communications network WPP, and we worked very closely with Jon Steel and the WPP Fellowship at the time. This opportunity was presented to a group of Fellows that were applying for a place on our programme and in 2013 Sarah Walker sent in her application and was accepted. Back then Sarah ran a Global Neuroscience Practice for the WPP network, and for 30 days she 'swapped the world of brains, behaviour and brands for a new kind of challenge': to fight the human rights abuses occurring during the preparations for the 2014 FIFA World Cup.

The team grew when Sarah arrived; a local agency run by a team of advertising students at a local university got involved, and together Sarah and the team worked with the Comitê to find solutions to the challenges faced. They all agreed that the main objective was to plan and launch a communications campaign that would help secure fair compensation from the government for all of the families and businesses forced out of their homes, and it was decided that there were two main mechanisms that could motivate the government to change their stance and support these people.

The first was FIFA imposing sanctions and punishing governments for exploitations of human rights in the name of the World Cup. Knowing FIFA, the short time frame, the number of contacts at FIFA (none) and significantly limited budget (£1,000), the chances of influence at this stage were limited. But we will come back to this option later.

The second option that could motivate the government to change their stance was to make the government fear that by not acting, they risked losing public support. This was key. The state governor was hoping to run for President of Brazil, and losing public votes was not something he could afford at that moment in his campaign. The team set out to make him fear that continuing with the current stance would lose him all-important votes.

They got to work and garnered widespread, highly visible support for a pressure campaign urging the government to pay fairer compensation to those it has displaced. The extra challenge was that news and media in Brazil are largely state controlled. As a result, there were no opportunities to be able to buy advertising space or get any PR coverage; the team had to think creatively and generate their own media.

They started by creating a campaign for people to unite under the same banner. It was called 'Nos Valemos Mais' – 'We're worth more'; a message to unite a city and let the government know that when they treat any of their citizens poorly, they harm everyone. Then the team created digital hubs around the city where people could share information. They captured people's real stories and turned these into images that could be shared. Then, they made the buildings the star; they photographed abandoned buildings waiting to be demolished and used them as the backdrops for the campaign. Taking this another step further, they used the buildings marked for eviction near busy bus routes as free outdoor media to graffiti their 'Nos Valemos Mais' messages on to (with the owner's permission of course). They even created a visual beach protest, getting up in the middle of the night to erect installations in popular middle-class beaches and parks to drive awareness of the evictions. They then took along iPads to get people to sign up to the campaign there and then.[14]

The campaign spread quickly. Within 72 hours their Facebook posts had been served to 90,000 people in Recife; 90,000 people who almost certainly didn't know about what was happening before.

But this was just the beginning. Although local awareness of the issues was raised by the end of Sarah's experience through the various campaigns created over her 30-day programme, it was clear that it wasn't enough for the principal local actors in this story, which involved the media, the government and the politicians, to take action against the human rights atrocities that were unfolding.

Once back in London Sarah started to look for more leverage, and the solution came down to the private sector. The moment that she started to connect the dots between risk, authenticity and corporate involvement in these types of events, things became more possible; she saw an untapped opportunity.

While local NGOs and pressure groups can lobby governments from the ground up, only FIFA really has the power to enforce any standards on any great scale, and at the time, there was nothing motivating them to do this. But Sarah realized, if their major corporate backers started to care, the situation would change rapidly. Sarah used her knowledge to bring the private sector into the equation for the good of society.

The idea that Sarah unearthed from her time in Brazil was that sponsors have the power to make FIFA act; this was Sarah's second line of attack. The global research company that she ran worked with many of the major global sponsors of FIFA and the World Cup in multiple markets and she wondered if there was an opportunity to use their relationships with those clients to highlight the risks to brands of being associated with such atrocities.

'If brands knew the risks to their reputations, would it encourage them to take more responsibility as sponsors of these events in the future?'

Sarah Walker

She decided to run a study that looked at measuring people's instinctive feelings towards the 2014 World Cup and the brands that sponsored it. They wanted to understand the impact that association with negative publicity around the World Cup can have on a brand. The results were shocking.

The data showed that by the end of the tournament, virtually everyone in Brazil was aware of issues around corruption and the expense of the tournament – and well over half had heard of forced relocations! Even outside of Brazil, awareness of the negative issues was growing with international pressure mounting on FIFA to take more action. Crucially, the studies showed the potential negative impacts of the increasing awareness of issues like corruption and political dishonesty on people's perceptions of the brands that link themselves to the tournament.

It illustrated that brands need to take an active stand advocating on behalf of the people, rather than being on the sidelines in cases of corruption and human rights abuses. As public pressure grows for FIFA to do more to prevent such atrocities, people will increasingly look to the major global brands involved in the tournament to use their power to press for positive change – and will increasingly hold them to account where they don't.[15]

> *'Brands need to take a more proactive relationship with the event that consumers perceive them to be a part of.'*
>
> Sarah Walker

The local knowledge around the human rights violations collected from Brazil and Sarah's research gave her and her team the opportunity to talk to their clients about brand risk and how sponsoring a questionable event can backfire. It also provided them with the opportunity to start conversations about the motivations for private sector companies to add pressure on behalf of affected communities and do what is possible to authentically and actively prevent similar social atrocities from happening in the future.

Although it wasn't a perfect outcome because all of the displaced people were not fairly compensated, global human rights organizations in partnership with the private sector pushed FIFA to form an advisory panel to instruct them on all issues related to the responsibility to uphold human rights in all future tournament staging.[16]

This strategy in 2007 wouldn't have been possible had Sarah not been exposed to such injustice. As well, the relationships created, and uncomfortable realities witnessed, brought out the best version of her leadership. It struck a chord, and she was compelled to do something about it. There is still a lot more that FIFA needs to do to play a dynamic role in standing up for human rights, but with private sector companies playing an ever more important role in driving positive change in social and environmental global issues, I believe further change is possible.

The result wasn't just a powerful strategy that added real value to Sarah's business and the global clients they served at the time, but by reaching outside of her usual network and creating a much bigger and influential community, Sarah and the team together, across sectors and countries, touched various people's lives in a meaningful way.

Bringing out the best of people through accountability

Life chances in Malawi aren't very common, but when people are given the correct tools to rebuild their lives, a meaningful new future can be created. Although primary school education in Malawi is free, not all children have the luxury of going to school for several reasons. Many couples have six or seven offspring, so not all children end up having the opportunity to be educated. Malawi is also one of the poorest countries in the world, leaving poverty levels high, and the result of this context is young children being forced to work in order to help bring money into the homes. School becomes an impossibility.[17]

The rates of HIV and Aids are also high. Many children are forced into becoming the heads of their households due to the death of their parents or guardians, leaving them with minimal or no support. These children have little choice but to take to the streets and do whatever they can to survive to look after their younger siblings. The result of all of this is high rates of petty crime.

The juvenile justice system in Malawi faces many challenges and children and young people in prisons often live in very difficult conditions. Judges in the Malawian Criminal Justice system have little or no option, once guilt is established, they must award a custodial sentence. Also, there are few, if any, viable alternatives to a jail sentence after a guilty plea and offenders are imprisoned often for minor offences. Unless the person is rich and has the means to simply buy their way out of prison, once the individual is found guilty, they will be one of the many stuck in prison for an unforeseeable length of time.

This is of course a recipe for disaster, and it's understandable why the prisons are overcrowded, with a disproportionately large population of poor children and young people. Incarcerated children have often been there for years; many can't remember when they started their sentence or even how old they are. They often go in healthy, but the conditions are so bad, they either die in jail or leave full of disease. People need to take it in turns to sleep, as the floor space can't fit everyone.

Chance for Change (C4C) is an organization that sees this as unacceptable. They work with young people who have experienced challenging living conditions when growing up and are ready for their transition to adulthood. They work in the UK, Malawi and Nepal, and enable young people with complicated life stories to become independent and take responsibility for their future direction. They see young people not as criminals, but instead as people with real value. Their goal is to rehabilitate former offenders while also preventing at-risk children from entering the formal judicial system in the first place.

One of the offerings that C4C provides is an Entrepreneurship Programme. This helps empower the young people to be their best by giving them the tools they need to rebuild their lives and then go on to run their own businesses and earn their own money. The initiative also transforms people from feeling unworthy to being worthwhile contributors to society with their work and ideas; it gives them a purpose to live and progress.

In 2018, the organization came to us looking for a specialist from the financial sector to help them improve on the programme. They needed someone to research what was working, what wasn't, and provide recommendations and implement solutions. This type of help is needed by many non-profits around the world as they often lack the people with the business skills to solve these types of issues.

This is when Chloe Allan got involved from the company Octopus Group. Octopus, a client of ours, was looking for opportunities to help their employees learn and grow in new ways and to use their business skills in different contexts. It was a perfect match. Chloe was a Business Development Manager for Octopus at the time, and on arrival in Malawi she wasted no time settling into her programme. She met George, Head of Entrepreneurship at C4C, who wanted to understand how the organization could be more effective. Very quickly Chloe's observations proved valuable. She noticed that many young people would learn a skill such as baking or farming but didn't have the money for the ingredients or the equipment to start a new enterprise. Of all the people she met, she felt that around half of them could have gone on to run a successful business had they been given the funding.

The next thing Chloe needed to do was understand how much it cost to start a small business in Malawi. After some field research, asking how much money people thought it would take to get their business going, she got her answer: around £15 to £20 per person. This was the information she needed to start finding tangible solutions that could help.

One of the solutions she came to was creating, for the first time, a loan facility for the programme. This would help the programme participants put everything they had learned into action. When the organization agreed with her thinking, she kept going. She discovered a local bank that historically lent to young enterprises and in the past had trialled two ways to lend – individually and in groups. When Chloe spoke with the bank manager who offered these loans in the past, she discovered that the default rate was considerably lower within groups, so the team realized that was the best way forward.

Then it all came to fruition. A year after Chloe's time in Malawi in 2019, and as a result of the loan solution that she and the team created, C4C lent 500,000 kwachas split equally across five groups, which amounted to £100 per group, and provided the start-up capital for 17 businesses.

I personally found the community loaning model fascinating, especially considering such a small number of companies defaulted on the loans; I was keen to understand how it worked. Chloe explained that it was the power of accountability that created the foundation of the lending strategy and that many other programmes work on the same principle. When people make a public promise to themselves, it's much more likely to work; if someone is looking to stop smoking, or write a book, or borrow money, it works in the same way.

The loan groups were chosen via a rigorous process and had to pass through several stages to pitch for the loan; once chosen, the entire group was responsible for the others. Therefore, if one person defaulted or stole the money, the group was much more likely to get them to pay. As a result, people felt more accountable. Also, the local Malawian community is tight and everyone knows one another; this helped to further ensure the success of this type of loan facility.

What this example shows is what is possible when you put people at the centre of an initiative. Yes, Chloe's financial understanding and perspective was helpful when it came to finding an impactful solution for the programme, but she would not have discovered that solution had she not sought after and intentionally connected with the local people; something the famous well-intentioned group never did when planting tomatoes in Zambia, mentioned in Chapter 1.

Chloe actively asked and listened to the local realities, and the result was an innovative and creative solution that impacted people's lives. She illustrated that one's ability to innovate and impact others doesn't necessarily depend on what that person knows, but rather their capacity to think out of the box and their aptitude to effectively work with others from different backgrounds.

Shrinking divides to make the world more human

'It takes a village to raise a child.'

African proverb[18]

A powerful consequence of working with people from dissimilar backgrounds is the discovery of a common humanity. Just before the pandemic I met Sam Theobald, Chief People Officer at the company Next15, a group of businesses from around the world designed to help companies grow. Sam is originally from Australia but has been living in the UK for years. In her role, she's known for working with entrepreneurial leaders and bringing a strong commercial edge to the HR function within companies, helping businesses grow. She knows that it's possible to have a commercial focus and still put people first.

When borders opened again in 2022 Sam took me for lunch, and we met in London to talk about collaborating. She was aware of a handful of people from around the corporate network that were looking for more purpose, connection and a desire to step outside of the day-to-day running of business, and knew she had to act fast; their excitement was flagging, and they needed to have the fire in their bellies reignited. Not long after, we had pulled together a group of senior leaders from around the company to take part in one of our virtual cohort programmes: two MDs – Liz based in Hong Kong and Karen in Sydney; a regional creative director, Lee, in Singapore; and Sam, based in London. All of them expats.

Together they decided to work with one of our partners in Kenya. Education was important to all of them, and no one came into the programme knowing much about the challenges that public schools face in the country. Quickly they learned that due to various factors, most students from public schools lack access to psychosocial and financial support to buy materials and that co-curricular activities and learning facilities are really overstretched. They also discovered that a major reason for youth unemployment in Kenya is due to poor awareness of available jobs, and there is a mismatch between the skills acquired at school and the skills needed in the 21st century labour market.

It was also made clear to them that this doesn't have to be the case. With a total of 38,194 primary and high schools in Kenya and generations of graduates from these institutions across all walks of life, there is a huge pool of human and financial resource that schools are not tapping into.[19] Their Alumni.

> 'Parents can't do it alone. Teachers can't do it alone. Alumni have to step up. Whether it's giving your former school a tin of paint or serving on the School Board, it doesn't matter how you give back; what is more important is that you do.'

The Late Ken Okoth,
Kenyan Member of Parliament and education advocate[20]

This is where organizations like Future First come in, and why they got in touch with me and my company TIE. They are experts in connecting and building the capacity of public school alumni as relatable role models who can provide mentorship, career guidance, scholarship and governance support to their former schools. Over the years they have seen the power of alumni in action, but they weren't reaching enough people. They needed help to engage more individuals with their former schools and create a best practice for alumni campaigns that can be tailored for implementation in other East African countries. Again, they knew what they needed, but required help from people in the business world to make it possible.

This was when the magic started to happen. Once we paired the global Next15 team with Future First Kenya, their common humanity was ignited.

The TIE programme called not only for business strategy and communication campaign development expertise, it also required the softer skills of compassion, empathy and openness so they could connect between themselves across borders, but also come up with a suitable solution for Kenyan children. Never had the Next15 professionals worked on a project that would impact so many people around a nation in such a human way. Although there were reservations at first about having a team from several continents, the professionals bonded as they worked together across countries, departments and sectors, and because it was a meaningful objective, they felt collectively connected to it; this construction prompted them to learn more about one another.

The brief was clear. The team needed to get alumni audiences to see that giving back to their school and community was part of their role in life by giving them reasons to care. Success equated to an increase of brand awareness for Future First, a pipeline of emails being generated and an increase of fundraising, sponsorships and mentorships.

The wheels were in motion and the team came together from around the world to position Future First as the conductor of a social movement that alumni wanted to be a part of. They were driven by the African proverb 'It takes a village to raise a child', and their version of this was that 'it takes a whole community to act and stand together to raise the next generation'. This became the focus of not only the work they created for the organization, but also the take aways from their programme.

#MyFuturePledge was born, which is a message to the next generation, saying that they vow to put them first and help them become the leaders of tomorrow. Through strategy development and numerous communication materials, the team created everything needed to start a new alumni movement and help the organization launch nationally. The call to action is an invitation for all alumni across Kenya to understand the power they have to make real change in their country; it's emotive, rooted in a truth that is impossible to ignore, and accessible. To join the movement people can easily pay it forward in time, materials or money.

Not only did Future First love the campaign, but the County of Nairobi Education Board bought into the idea and agreed it was a movement that needed to be created. They promised to back the campaign with all government goodwill, which is considered to be the best press possible. Although the next phase of turning the campaign into something tangible hasn't been easy, the wheels are still in motion. Pauline, Future First's CEO, presented to the National Media Group team, and to an advisor at the Office of a Special Initiative at the Office of the President, and the advisor has gone beyond the call of duty to ensure the request gets the audience it deserves; from the Office of the Permanent Secretary to the Office of the Prime Cabinet Secretary and the Permanent Secretary of Education, amongst others. The launch is imminent and the organization is 'revelling in the new possibilities'. A very exciting moment.

But our work has always been a win–win, and the purpose of these programmes is to impact professionals and their leadership as much as the non-profit organizations. This programme managed to get very senior professionals to see themselves and their work in a different light. They finished the experience still being expats living abroad but found themselves reflecting on how similar each member of the team was, no matter where they were all from, and as a result better appreciated the importance of creating global connections and common bonds. This is the result of discovering a common humanity.

Once the team recognized the power and importance of coming together with passion and conviction to find a successful solution that made an impact, they came out with different visions of themselves and their work, more purpose, new-found confidence and more effective ways of working. This was a chance to create more interpersonal relationships around different markets, more collaboration throughout the Next15 network, and walk the walk when it comes to purpose. Everyone managed to drop into a different presence, experienced themselves in new ways and unleashed an untouched part of their humanity.

Finding that common humanity and understanding the power of crossing divides is a major way to making the world more human. Once we unlock this in leaders, there is no going back.

———————

The objective of this chapter was to show that there are numerous people in various markets around the world facing similar challenges. Once leaders understand the power of crossing divides and finding a common humanity with others, they will be a driving force to making the world a better place to live.

10

The opportunities out there waiting to be embraced

As I wrap up the book in this chapter, I reflect on what is needed to create a more sustainable world and respond to the turbulent environment around us. We are in the driver's seat when it comes to changing things and the answers come down to each one of us.

Creating ripples of possibility

Francisco José de Goya y Lucientes was considered one of the most important Spanish artists of the late 18th and early 19th centuries. But what he left behind wasn't only art that made a mark on contemporary culture with his technique and innovative thinking, it was also life lessons in humility. Before he died in France in 1828, he painted a small print of an elderly, long-bearded man hunched over two canes. In a conversation I had with UK strategist Jim Carroll, he reflected on this painting and said that many people believe that the sketch is of the artist, coming to the end of his life.[1]

Goya's life was hard; he witnessed the Peninsular War, went deaf and had to leave his beloved homeland. He struggled without any financial or moral support from his immediate family, and after studying art, rose to become the painter for the royal family. Goya experienced a lot in his life, yet at the top of this painting, he wrote 'Aun Aprendo', which means 'I'm still learning'. As Jim said, 'That is wisdom'.

Jim went on to say that as we get older and gain experience, we start to develop fixed points of view and perspectives. As we become more of an expert, it's easy to think we've learned what we need to learn, and then that's when we get siloed, stop being curious and no longer have doubt. One of the biggest challenges in leadership today is learning when you already know.

> 'In the judicial system we talk about "reasonable doubt", but what about "unreasonable certainty"? Total certainty is unreasonable.'
>
> *Jim Carroll*

But this inner development isn't just important for our own personal growth and the development of our own leadership competencies. It is what is required to create a more sustainable planet and future. I recently heard about the Nordic Secret, which beautifully illustrates why inner development is key to driving not only corporate and societal change, but also for reaching the sustainable development goals.

In Tomas Björkman's TED talk, he explains that just under 160 years ago Scandinavia looked very different to how it looks now.[2] It was poor, not democratic, there was no freedom of speech and their industry was in the process of moving from agrarian to industrial. It was a moment of real instability and disruption, and the leaders of Scandinavia at that time understood that the self-awareness and inner strength of the population were key to creating resilience and a stable region. This is because when groups of people go through significant change it creates unrest, leaving individuals feeling unsettled. When that happens, it opens opportunities for authoritarian leaders to feed on the fear and offer that external support – increasing their power. However, the more self-aware people are, the more centred they are. They see themselves clearly, are more confident and become less reliant on external variables; this makes it much harder for others to manipulate and control them.

The leaders of the region knew that to future proof Scandinavia, they needed to empower a large part of the population to be active co-creators of the new future and to create that stability. The result was the implementation of retreat centres for inner growth all over Scandinavia called folk high schools. From 1860 to 1900 the schools expanded across the region. Young adults would spend up to six months, free of charge (state funded, but not state run), with the sole objective of finding themselves and their inner compass; to become so stable inside that they could handle the complex societal transition externally. Then a few decades later, even before the Second World War, the region transitioned to become the happy, stable, industrialised and rich democracies they are known as today.[3]

When Erik Fernholm, Co-founder of the IDGs and 29k, told me about the Nordic Secret, he went on to tell me about a conversation he had a few years ago with former President Barack Obama.[4,5] They were at an event together and Obama said that if it wasn't for the folk high schools, he wouldn't have been president. He explained that in 1932, after seeing the success in Scandinavia, an American brought the folk high schools concept to the US and the centre was called the Highlander Folk School, which focused on social justice and leadership training, based in Monteagle, Tennessee.[6] Obama didn't study there, but someone did that shaped the future of the US and created the environment within which Obama could become president.

At 42 years of age, shortly after graduating from a two-week course at the Highlander Folk School, a young woman was on a bus. When she was asked to move and sit in another seat at the back, she didn't get up. Her name was Rosa Parks.[7]

'We would not have been here had it not been for that stone that was thrown in the lake and created ripples of hope that ultimately spread across the ocean to the United States of America. I might not be standing here were it not for the efforts of people like Ella Baker and the others who participated in the Highlander Folk School.'

President Barack Obama, at the Nordic State Dinner[8]

For people to be drivers of change and to respond to the turbulent environment around us, they must build inner strength and be inner directed. Neuroscience confirms the importance of this today, and this is the basis of the IDGs. We need this inner knowledge to be able to respond to what is going on around us, and we need it to be better leaders.

The IDGs were initiated and co-founded in 2020 by Erik Fernholm through the 29k Foundation, the Ekskäret Foundation and The New Division (the design firm that created the Sustainable Development Goals, or the SDGs, for the UN). Rooted in science and together with a large group of researchers, experts and practitioners in leadership development and sustainability, they have managed to prove the inner shifts or human growth required to reach the SDGs. In short, the skills leaders need to create a more sustainable future. Not surprisingly, the inner capacities are all rooted in human values, behaviours and skills.

The IDGs have identified 23 skills and separated them into five categories. The skills include ones such as inner compass, openness, learning mindset, self-awareness, presence, sense making, connectedness, humility, co-creating skills, trust, perseverance, resilience and more. Many of these are the human assets we have talked about throughout this book so far.

Andrew Bovarnick, Global Head Food and Agricultural Commodity systems, UNDP, complements this thinking by saying:

> '*I used to think that the top environmental problems were biodiversity loss, ecosystem collapse and climate change. I thought that with 30 years of good science, we could address those problems. But I was wrong. The top environmental problems are selfishness, greed and apathy.*'[9]

A significant cultural and social shift still needs to happen, and it comes down to every single one of us. This is a hopeful message. We are fully in control of the changes that need to be made, but if as a society we are only looking at success through the lens of financial wealth and material possessions, a sustainable future is impossible. The key is to work on our inner development, and the inner development of others, to ensure the necessary shifts happen.

If, as individuals, we are happy with who we are, and develop our inner skills and worth, then we become less dependent on the external variables, such as consumption and monetary things used to fill a void; that external noise simply goes away and no longer matters. It's having that inner strength of knowing who we are, having the wisdom to know that things need to be done differently and the courage to challenge the system to create new ways of operating in the world. This is the return on humanity and the power it has to create a more sustainable planet for us all.

These are turbulent times of transformation and transition. To be active conscious co-creators of the future that we want to emerge, we need to be inner directed and develop those inner human assets to be the drivers of that change.

If we can enable people at scale to recognize the power of their human assets, feel their sense of connectedness to themselves and the world, we can start to make societal shifts. Let's give people permission to see the power in humanity and choose leaders based on these values and behaviours or focus on unlocking these assets in ourselves and others.

Lessons from a hummingbird

> '*Only those who attempt the absurd will achieve the impossible.*'
>
> Miguel de Unamuno[10]

There is a beautiful indigenous parable of a hummingbird that challenges the idea that greatness is a prerequisite to success and creating a better future and highlights the belief in the power of small. You can hear this story throughout the Americas and it goes something like this:

'Once upon a time, there was a fire in the forest and all the animals were fleeing. All except the hummingbird. She was flying towards the fire with a drop of water in her beak. "Silly little bird," shouted the eagle, soaring above her, "Don't you realize you'll never put out the fire all by yourself?"

*The hummingbird flew on towards the fire and dropped the water. Then she looked up at the eagle. "You're right," she said, "I'll never do it by myself. But I'm doing my part."'[11]

Iracambi, one of our non-profit partners mentioned in Chapter 1, shared this with us, and I love the message (their logo is a hummingbird because of what this story represents); we can do our part to making things better, and every little bit counts.

It's easy to wonder if we are even capable of fixing things. We feel stuck, even scared, and at times almost want to bury our heads in the sand; if we just did that, maybe these challenges will all just go away. But finding that inner strength within us is what will help everything start to change course. There is a new movement coming, which we can all feel. We know that things need to be done differently and that change is vital; it's crucial that we realize that all of us, as a global community, ordinary citizens from around the world, can be a part of this shift. Change is in our hands.

In my mind, to create the conditions for change to happen doesn't need to be complicated:

o **First**: We need to acknowledge there is a problem that impacts the world around us.

We may have become so accustomed to the established way of working, living and being that we might miss opportunities where the addition of more humanity could make a difference to our everyday or professional lives. To spot those opportunities, we need to take a step back and assess our and other people's realities, including those that happen across borders. Being consciously aware of the world around us is a call to action to tap into our human assets from individual, business and global perspectives.

o **Second**: We need to be clear on what success means.

The traditional definition of success is very much associated with wealth, power and income, but what if we start defining it more in human and personal terms like developing a sense of accomplishment, pleasure and fulfilment through who we are and what we do.

It's important to question success because it's directly connected to failure. What does success mean to us as individuals and what does it mean in relation to companies in the whole scheme of things? We all know how easy it is to get side-tracked in life to what a fulfilling life really is, and therefore, what success should be. Is it money and status? Is it always reaching our predetermined goals? Should different time frames be considered? Does success involve failure?

Erik Fernholm, who I mentioned earlier, Co-founder of the IDGs and who has a background in Cognitive Neuroscience and Happiness Research, asks people that he's working with a simple question: 'When do you feel fulfilled?' He then asks them to think about what fulfilment looks like and if it's the same conclusion that they imagined success to be. Next, he has them find patterns of their lived experiences. When people reflect on this simple exercise, they often start to understand their values and realize what it means to be authentically successful.

When considering corporate success, time frames matter. Should companies measure success over three months, six months, a year, two years, or should they be building something that they are proud of and that makes the leaders feel good? If so, the time horizon to measure success needs to be decades and lifetimes, not months.

If success doesn't feel successful, you know you need to do some more thinking. That's why measuring success needs to be done correctly. When you do that, you then know where to spend your time and effort, ensuring it not only leads to a feeling of happiness and fulfilment in life, but also a more sustainable world.

○ **Finally**, we need to **act**.

We need to roll up our sleeves and do something because change won't come if we wait for someone else. Remember, as the stories in this book have illustrated, being able to change something doesn't require a certain position or education, and it doesn't depend on your postal code, social status or income level.

Throughout the three sections of this book, I have provided a number of different stories that highlight people from all walks of life, and they all have something in common; they have accessed their human assets and used them to impact the world around them. I included a wide range of stories because I wanted to show you that you can come from Kilimanjaro Tanzania, be a middle-class 80-year-old man who has only ever lived in Brazil, be a young woman from Iraq who has grown up in an oppressive regime, or an account director from New York. Everyone has human assets, and what this book is providing is a blueprint to understand those traits and how to access them. You can come from anywhere.

The key is to recognize the power you have at your fingertips: dream big and act.

As a child, I loved watching *The NeverEnding Story*. I must have watched it 20 times, but I'm not sure I truly understood the message until I watched it again as an adult. In 2023 I watched it with my girls, and the message I took out was this...

Don't underestimate the power of fantasy because we all need fantasy to achieve something. In fact, I would go as far as saying that one can't happen without the other. Without a dream, we don't have an objective or a reason to push ourselves. Without fantasy, the concrete world doesn't exist.

Nothing has happened without a dream, without a desire and someone to make it happen. So, dream big. Know that you can challenge the current reality and make the impossible, possible. Just go ahead and do it; that is the never-ending story.

A final challenge

'What if instead of trying to lead the best businesses in the world in your sectors, you shifted to trying to create the best businesses for the world. What new opportunities might open up for your stakeholders? What implications might there be for your business?'

Paul Skinner[12]

I've posed many challenges in this book about the current state of the world. Some of them include:

o   What if there was another way to think about business?

o   What if financials weren't the only predictor of success?

o   What if purely external solutions weren't the only way to solve global problems?

And throughout I've tried to provide some concrete solutions to help formulate the answers.

But now, I'd like to look to all of you reading.

You may be a leader in business, whatever form that may take. You may run your own company. You may be retired, but reflecting on how things could have been different had these concepts been considered when you were in business. Or perhaps you're a student hoping to shape a more positive future.

Whatever your background, it's important to know that change can still happen, and the power is in your hands. So, I'd like to challenge you once more as we start to wrap things up.

What if your job as a leader was to be open to finding new ways of doing things, and what if you were given permission to be vulnerable and bring humanity back to the equation?

This is about creating a future that you know is possible but hasn't yet arrived.

Where we were is different to where we are going, and the fundamentals of the system must be reinvented for a sustainable future to even be possible. As a society, we are all still searching for the answers to what that future looks like, but we do know it's a future that connects with our humanity.

There are a few ways that we can create this unknown vision that we know is possible, and there is one group of people that is fundamental to this change. These are intrapreneurs: employees who act like an entrepreneur but are working within a company. We know that the way the private sector works and behaves needs to evolve; this is essential to ensure the survival of companies and the health of the planet. But this change isn't coming from the top of companies; it's emerging from within by this group of people who know how the system works, have access to the resources, feel the urgency and want to do something about it. Intrapreneurs know change is risky for everyone involved; for the person driving it, as well as for the organizations involved in that change. But they look at the status quo, and it makes them feel uneasy. They are willing to take certain risks and interpret trends in the marketplace to visualize the next steps that a company may need to take and believe they can move the business forward by leveraging company assets to make their vision a reality.

As Gib Bulloch, award-winning social intrapreneur and author of *The Intrapreneur: Confessions of a Corporate Insurgent,* says, intrapreneurs are effective in driving change because they can bridge borders, network with different people and transcend adversity.[13] They can rally people behind a cause and build momentum behind their ideas. They are self-aware, flexible and lead from the heart. They are empathetic, embrace diversity, take calculated risks and are comfortable in uncomfortable situations. They can collaborate, gain the trust and buy-in from different actors around a company and think innovatively.[14]

Their skills are rooted in humanity.

> 'Don't change companies. Don't change industries. Change the company or industry you're in.'
>
> *Gib Bulloch*[15]

Anyone working at a company has the potential to be an intrapreneur, but the key is unlocking that human potential to make being an intrapreneur a success.

What if companies invest more in training leaders' humanity so they can lead teams, companies and the world in the right direction?

More human companies are only possible if they are run by, and filled with, people who have tapped into the power of their humanity. The world is crying out for people who are kinder and more thoughtful, as well as for companies that make you feel good and put people and planet first.

This is why unlocking people's humanity is so important, and it's by experiencing life in new ways that allows this to happen. But just wanting to make the world work better isn't enough; the key is the right kind of training and exposure to create the necessary transformation to unlock not only the right thinking, but also the appropriate skills and then behaviours. This is what I've been doing with my work over the past two decades and what I have illustrated with stories throughout this book.

Over the years leaders have discovered how to both think and feel, become comfortable in ambiguous situations and learned to remain flexible and empathetic. They became professionals wanting to challenge the status quo and fight for more human and responsible business practices.

But this growth is the responsibility of everyone involved. Individuals need to have the courage and make the time and investment to see the world in new ways and push themselves to think, lead and work differently. Equally, companies must recognize not only that people want to be a part of this movement to a more human way of working, but that the insights, innovative thinking and creativity developed from stepping into new realities and being pushed contributes significant value to a business.

Finally, what if each of us becomes aware of the unique human assets we possess and translate them into meaningful actions and strategies?

I'm optimistic.

Throughout the year, every couple of weeks, I have the luxury of speaking to people on my podcast who are challenging the system. Each one of them are disruptors, united by a common goal: to bring their purpose to life. They may come from the commercial world, third sector or public sector. They may come from the Global North or the Global South. But what they have in common is that they have all made it their mission to upset the apple cart and have proven that anything is possible.

On one episode I spoke to a friend of mine, Ben Akers, who set up an organization called Talk Club, a talking and listening charity for men.[16] He set it up with the simple mission to decrease the number of men taking their own lives.

What struck me about this organization wasn't how incredible it is (because it is incredible); but what got me was its business model. Talk Club is a charity, but being a charity doesn't mean that you need to create a revenue model that relies on handouts or grants. When I spoke to Ben, he explained that he's in the business of human sustainability; but he didn't want to create an organization based on the regular system. So, he found another way of working.

He decided to partner with brands and create products where customers can be purposeful with their purchases. They started by talking with the Bristol Beer Factory and asked if they were interested in creating Clear Head, a non-alcoholic beer. The idea was that Talk Club would get 5% of the profits from that. Ben explained that even though they turned him down three times, it's now the Bristol Beer Factory's biggest selling beer. 'They can't actually make it quick enough,' he told me.

This is a win–win for both organizations. Ben has now started to do this with other brands too and things are going from strength to strength. They are using a product to create an important conversation, but using that conversation to help fuel the charity. The power of collaboration, thinking differently and challenging old models.

Then there is Alex Garden who spent eight years challenging the plastic packaging industry.

Any food that moves must use packaging, and the global packaging market accounts for over US$1 trillion annually. Single-use consumer plastic packaging alone is US$340 billion and results in 190 million tons of plastic produced a year.[17] To put this into perspective, Alex told me that there is so much residual plastic in our food and water that each of us consumes about the equivalent of a credit card's worth per week, and the UN estimates that by 2050 there will be more plastic in the world's oceans than fish.[18] But plastic isn't the only option, and there are packaging solutions beyond plastic with price and performance parity. Alex made it his mission for almost a decade to find plastic packaging alternatives that are available at scale and able to service the biggest brands in the world.

There are also so many other fantastic packaging solutions popping up from various entrepreneurs around the world. There is Gigs 2 Go, credit card-sized flash drives made from recycled paper pulp; an idea that started as a bit of a blue-sky concept, but then when the founders started talking about it publicly, and collaborated with others for feedback and financial resources, they managed to make it into production.[19] There is also Kaffeeform, a company that takes the concept of the circular economy to a new level. They take renewable resources such as used coffee grounds and recycled beechwood scraps and upcycle them. The result is durable, robust and sustainable everyday packaging solutions that look gorgeous.[20]

Then there are the numerous other businesses around the world that are rooted in the concept of the Circular Economy which works by simply promoting the regenerative model of make–use–return, an important solution that helps to decrease the problem of resource scarcity and waste overload. Around the world people are talking about the importance for collaboration between all sectors to create more circular economy solutions in every industry.

The list goes on when it comes to innovative solutions to challenging the status quo, and many of the groundbreaking solutions needed to improve our global situation are still waiting to be invented.

For this to happen we all need to remember that a better world where individuals, businesses and society all prosper is only possible if we go back to basics and return humanity to the equation. The biggest change will come from more human businesses because they have the greatest potential to change the world for the better; they have the financial and human resources as well as the reach.

It's more important now than ever before for us to realize that we are all capable of doing incredible things that will change the world, that will create the positive returns we need to turn things around, and we are the ones we've been waiting for.

'The opposite of courage in our society is not cowardice, it is conformity.'

Rollo May[21]

An invitation

We make so many decisions these days that force us to look at the returns: the return on time investment, on financial investment and so on. But as we've seen in this book, the reality is that when humanity isn't at the core of something, it's expensive, in all senses of the word: employees aren't happy and leave companies (or file lawsuits); social interactions are horrible and therefore leave people feeling worse off; customer experiences are bad, and therefore they don't return; and the ability to reach the sustainable development goals becomes almost impossible.

Everything points back to being more human and tapping into those human values and skills, and once we start to see things through that lens, we see that things in general improve. We get better people, better companies and, as a result, a better world.

The way to create change is by injecting more humanity into all we do; how we behave as people and how we run our companies. It's about being curious, asking questions and listening more than you speak, even if it's difficult. It's about bringing people, communities and countries together. It's about courage and bridge building.

Humans are at the core of all our global problems today, but that is a message of hope. It means that we are in the driver's seat when it comes to changing things. The revolution of our time is realizing that we now must focus on our humanity.

This is about developing our sense of connectedness to ourselves and to others around the world, and surrendering to the fact that we need to constantly develop to be in touch with ourselves, to raise our consciousness, to grow and become more human. It's also about getting companies to align to this thinking, and either choose leaders based on human capacities, or help their leaders develop them.

'Today is the last day of our lives that things are moving this slowly, and what people do in these moments between world chapters matters.'

Erik Fernholm[22]

I believe that everyone reading this book has the ability to impact the quality of life for the next generation, no matter your age, your position, background or industry.

The world needs what you have. You have more power than you think you do. The time is now.

Author's notes

Thank you for coming on my journey and please let me know what you think of the book by writing a brief online review https://mybook.to/ReturnOnHumanity

If you'd like to join me on my adventures follow @TIEleadership on Instagram or you can find me on LinkedIn at Philippa White.

Should you wish to book me for a speaking engagement or deliver a keynote at a conference, please visit my website philippajwhite.com to find out more. I look forward to hearing from you.

And if you'd like to improve the performance of your leaders and teams or see how we can work together, check out tieleadership.com

Thanks so much again for reading my book and here's to injecting more humanity into life and business.

Philippa

Acknowledgements

We are all a result of our collective experiences. This book would not have been possible without so many people who have not only touched me throughout my life – both good and bad – but who also worked so hard to help make this book possible. For that I am so grateful.

I want to say thank you to my parents for being such incredible role models. The love they had for one another, for my siblings and me, and the lessons they gave us have provided much of the foundation of the thinking here. A special shout out to my Mum who is, to this day, not only that voice of reason I rely on so much, but one of the most just, thoughtful and toughest people I know. Bia and Maya, you teach me so much daily. Thank you for making me better. Guga, thank you for the constant inspiration, love and support. This book would not have been possible without your invaluable perspective. Gilmara Jerônimo dos Santos, without question, none of this would have been logistically possible without you. You're part of the family. Justine Quince, thank you for allowing me to share your and Neil's stories, for taking the time to capture the specific details and providing me with the perspective that shaped the trajectory of my life. Ines Vogeler, your patience, dedication and constant support and belief in TIE and all we do is so appreciated. Your strategic push, relentless questioning with love and passion for this subject helped turn this book into what it is today. I also don't know if I would have managed to crack the structure and flow without you. Thank you for being so kind and tough and for dedicating that incredible brain of yours to this project! Ulle Figueiredo, thank you for constantly pushing me when I think I know the answers and for your detective work when it came to the job of references. Harry MacAuslan, for years you have been there supporting me and TIE. Your support is invaluable, but specifically if it wasn't for you, we wouldn't have the subtitle nor cracked the intro. Eternally grateful for your ability to cut through the noise and find those nuggets. Nick Hastings, thank you for your words and creativity. Paul Steggall, thank you for ensuring I don't give up and for those phone calls of support. They hold so much power. Juliana Menucci, thank you for your contributions to the book when it came to my international development doubts. Peter Herbert and Matt Symonds, the phone calls and direction over the last year have helped get us to this stage. Thank you. Michael Jager, thank you not only for the various stories and contacts that helped contribute to the ideas in the book, but also for your direction, patience and design skills to help create the cover. To all of the contributors to the book – your perspectives and stories have been invaluable and made it what it is. Clearly a book on humanity needed a host of different voices, and I'm so lucky to have all of you in my life. Also, a huge shout out to the various proofreaders and people who helped with book development. This has been a group effort: Harry MacAuslan, Ed Mayo, Ines Vogeler, Ulle Figueiredo, Josh Governale, Senta Slingerland, Juliana Xavier, Whitney Clapper and Binka le Breton. Alison Jones, thank you for managing to draw this book out of me; you have an incredible talent. And a special shout out to Eliot and Claire Postma for being my home away from home. Please note, although this has been a very participatory process, if there are any errors here, they are mine alone.

Notes

Introduction: A leader driven by his humanity

1   Passing of Activist Prof Neil White. www.news.uct.ac.za/article/-2004-11-15-passing-of-activist-prof-neil-white [accessed 26 September 2023].

2   NAMDA (National Medical and Dental Association) was a non-racial progressive organization of South African doctors. H.M. Coovadia 'Sanctions and the Struggle for Health in South Africa' in *American Journal of Public Health*, 89 (10/October) 1505–08 (1999). doi:10.2105/A8JPH.89.10.1505

3   The UDF (United Democratic Front) was a mass democratic movement that emerged in the mid-1980s to lead the internal struggle against apartheid. *United Democratic Front (UDF) – The O'Malley Archives.* https://omalley.nelsonmandela.org/index.php/site/q/03lv02424/04lv02730/05lv03188/06lv03222.htm [accessed 7 July 2023].

4   IsiXhosa is one of the 11 official languages recognized by the South African Constitution, spoken by over 7 million South Africans. Xhosa – South African History Online. www.sahistory.org.za/article/xhosa [accessed 14 July 2023].

5   Hansard – Parliament of South Africa. www.parliament.gov.za/hansard?queries%5bsearch%5d=2004 [accessed 26 September 2023].

6   'Only 11 years left to prevent irreversible damage from climate change, speakers warn during General Assembly High-Level Meeting' in *UN Press.* https://press.un.org/en/2019/ga12131.doc.htm [accessed 26 September 2023].

Chapter 1: The special human ingredients

1   Früh übt sich, wer ein Meister werden will – German proverb. 'früh übt
     sich, wer ein Meister werden will.' Wiktionary (22 December 2022).
     https://de.wiktionary.org/w/index.php?title=fr%C3%BCh_%C3%BCbt_
     sich,_wer_ein_Meister_werden_will&oldid=9469922

2   Erik Olsen 'Sailing around the world for eight years with three kids
     taught us to live without structure' in *Quartz* (8 October 2016). https://
     qz.com/778593/sailing-around-the-world-for-eight-years-with-three-
     kids-taught-us-to-live-without-structure

3   'Helping kids with flexible thinking' in Child Mind Institute. https://
     childmind.org/article/helping-kids-with-flexible-thinking/ [accessed 9
     May 2023].

4   Anaïs Nin and Anita Jarczok *Seduction of the Minotaur*. Swallow Press/Ohio
     University Press (2014).

5   Ernesto Sirolli 'Want to Help Someone? Shut up
     and Listen!' 1353946523. www.ted.com/talks/
     ernesto_sirolli_want_to_help_someone_shut_up_and_listen

6   Ernesto Sirolli 'Want to Help Someone? Shut up
     and Listen!' 1353946523. www.ted.com/talks/
     ernesto_sirolli_want_to_help_someone_shut_up_and_listen

7   Voltaire. Letter to Frederick the Great (28 November 1770).

8   Sydney Finkelstein 'Don't be blinded by your own expertise' in
     Harvard Business Review (May 2019). https://hbr.org/2019/05/
     dont-be-blinded-by-your-own-expertise

9   Brené Brown 'The power of vulnerability.' 1293115500. www.ted.com/
     talks/brene_brown_the_power_of_vulnerability/c/transcript

10   Julia Middleton *Cultural Intelligence: CQ: The Competitive Edge for Leaders
     Crossing Borders*. Bloomsbury Academic (2014).

11   Michelangelo et al. *Complete Poems and Selected Letters of Michelangelo*.
     Edited by Robert N. Linscott, Princeton paperback print. Princeton
     University Press (1980).

12   'Y2K bug' in *National Geographic*. https://education.nationalgeographic.
     org/resource/Y2K-bug [accessed 5 February 2023].

13   MAR Fund – Protecting the Mesoamerican Reef. https://marfund.org/
     en/ [accessed 6 June 2023].

14   'Brazilian Amazon Deforestation up 150% in Bolsonaro's last
     month' in Aljazeera. www.aljazeera.com/news/2023/1/7/

brazilian-amazon-deforestation-up-150-in-bolsonaros-last-month [accessed 7 February 2023].

15 'What are the biggest drivers of tropical deforestation?' in *World Wildlife Fund.* www.worldwildlife.org/magazine/issues/summer-2018/articles/ what-are-the-biggest-drivers-of-tropical-deforestation [accessed 6 February 2023].

16 Iracambi. https://iracambi.com/ [accessed 5 February 2023].

17 Jiyan Foundation for Human Rights. https://jiyan.org/ [accessed 6 June 2023].

18 Philippa White. *Ep:#62 The Force of Self-Awareness in Iraq with Asmaa Ibrahim and Jiyan Foundation.* https://tieleadership.com/podcast/the-force-of-self-awareness-in-iraq-with-asmaa-ibrahim-and-jiyan-foundation/

Chapter 2: What liberates our human assets?

1 Interview with Climber Alex Honnold on Risk, Choice and God. 'Adventure' in *National Geographic* (30 December 2015). www.nationalgeographic.com/adventure/article/ ropeless-climber-alex-honnolds-closest-call

2 Sir John Hegarty and Philippa White *Sir John Hegarty and Philippa White's 6 Tips on How to Unleash Your True Potential.* The International Exchange – Internal Document (2022).

3 Sir John Hegarty and Philippa White *Sir John Hegarty and Philippa White's 6 Tips on How to Unleash Your True Potential.* The International Exchange – Internal Document (2022).

4 Sir John Hegarty and Philippa White *Sir John Hegarty and Philippa White's 6 Tips on How to Unleash Your True Potential.* The International Exchange – Internal Document (2022).

5 Sara Tate and Anna Vogt *The Rebuilders: Going from Setback to Comeback in Business and Beyond.* Kogan Page (2022).

6 Eleanor Roosevelt *You Learn by Living: Eleven Keys for a More Fulfilling Life.* 50th anniversary edn, HarperPerennial: Publishers Group UK [distributor] (2012).

7 Philippa White. *Ep:#51 Going from Setback to Comeback with Sara Tate.* https://tieleadership.com/podcast/ going-from-setback-to-comeback-with-sara-tate/

8 Keridwen Cornelius, 'Biosphere 2: The once infamous live-in terrarium is transforming climate research' in *Scientific American.* www.

scientificamerican.com/article/biosphere-2-the-once-infamous-live-in-terrarium-is-transforming-climate-research/ [accessed 26 September 2023].

9   Philippa White. *Ep:#34 Michael Jager on Designing Brands People Actually Love.* https://tieleadership.com/podcast/michael-jager-on-designing-brands-people-actually-love/

10   Philippa White. *Ep:#34 Michael Jager on Designing Brands People Actually Love.* https://tieleadership.com/podcast/michael-jager-on-designing-brands-people-actually-love/

11   Warren Bennis and Robert J. Thomas 'Crucibles of leadership' in *Harvard Business Review* (September 2002). https://hbr.org/2002/09/crucibles-of-leadership

12   Wayne W. Dyer *Change Your Thoughts, Change Your Life: Living the Wisdom of the Tao.* Hay House (2010).

13   'What is Wabi Sabi? The Elusive Beauty of Imperfection' in *Japan Objects* (8 January 2021). https://japanobjects.com/features/wabi-sabi

14   The 14th Dalai Lama 'Dealing with negative emotions' in The 14th Dalai Lama (25 May 2023). www.dalailama.com/videos/dealing-with-negative-emotions

15   Epictetus and Robert F. Dobbin *Discourses and Selected Writings.* Penguin (2008).

16   Paulo Freire 'Não há educação neutra' in acervo.paulofreire.org:8080 (May 1977). http://acervo.paulofreire.org:8080/xmlui/handle/7891/1283

17   Md. Mahbubul Alam 'Banking model of education in teacher-centered class: A critical assessment' in *Research on Humanities and Social Sciences*, 3 (5), (2013).

18   Philippa White. *Ep:#61 Rick Wheatley on Breaking out of the Old Ways of Thinking to Create the Future We Need.* https://tieleadership.com/podcast/rick-wheatley-on-breaking-out-of-the-old-ways-of-thinking-to-create-the-future-we-need/

19   'Inner development goals' in Inner Development Goals. https://www.innerdevelopmentgoals.org [accessed 26 June 2023].

20   *David Bowie: The Last Five Years.* Directed by Francis Whately (2017). www.imdb.com/title/tt6375308/

21   Sara Tate and Anna Vogt *The Rebuilders: Going from Setback to Comeback in Business and Beyond.* Kogan Page (2022).

Chapter 3: The impact of using human assets

1   Instagram. Cozinhas Afetivas. www.instagram.com/cozinhasafetivas/ [accessed 13 April 2023].

2   Philippa White. *Ep:#62 The Force of Self-Awareness in Iraq with Asmaa Ibrahim and Jiyan Foundation*. https://tieleadership.com/podcast/ the-force-of-self-awareness-in-iraq-with-asmaa-ibrahim-and-jiyan-foundation/

3   'IDG framework' in Inner Development Goals. www. innerdevelopmentgoals.org/framework [accessed 13 April 2023].

4   1913 Natives Land Act Centenary – South African Government. www.gov.za/1913-natives-land-act-centenary#:~:text=The%20Act%20 became%20law%20on,employees%20of%20a%20white%20master [accessed 13 June 2023].

5   Nulda Beyers and Eric Bateman 'Obituary. Neil White (15 May 1954 – 6 November 2004)' in *The International Journal of Tuberculosis and Lung Disease (IJTLD)*, 9 (3), 351 (2005). www.ingentaconnect.com/content/ iuatld/ijtld/2005/00000009/00000003/art00023?crawler=true

6   Brendan V. Girdler-Brown et al. 'The burden of silicosis, pulmonary tuberculosis and COPD among former Basotho goldminers' in *American Journal of Industrial Medicine*, 51 (9/September), 640–47 (2008). doi:10.1002/ajim.20602

7   Neil White 'Silicosis: What is to be done?' in Theme Paper, Division of Occupational Medicine. University of Cape Town and Groote Schuur Hospital (2004).

8   Neil White 'Is the ODMW Act fair? A Comparison of the Occupational Diseases in Mines and Works Amendment Act, 1993 and the Compensation of Occupational Injuries and Diseases Act, 1993 with respect to compensation of pneumoconiosis' in Occasional Monograph, Centre for Occupational and Environmental Health Research, 1–31. University of Cape Town (2004).

9   'S.A. Health and Safety Standards "decades behind"' in *FOSATU Worker News*, p. 3, (September 1983). www.sahistory.org.za/sites/default/files/ archive-files/FwSep83.1562.7624.000.024.Sep1983.9.pdf

10 Philippa White. *Ep:#68 Life after Spinal Cord Injury in Africa with Faustina Urassa*. https://tieleadership.com/podcast/ life-after-spinal-cord-injury-in-africa-with-faustina-urassa/

11 Values and Principles – UNESCO Chair GHE. https://unescochair-ghe. org/the-unesco-chair-ghe/values-and-principles/ [accessed 17 March 2023].

12   Arthur Smith. *The Present Situation for Writing and Publishing Creative Writing for Children in Africa* (2014). http://www.arthureesmith.net/ [accessed 11 November 2014].

Chapter 4: The problem with old business paradigms

1   Hannah Arendt *The Origins of Totalitarianism*. New edn, Harcourt Brace Jovanovich (1973).

2   Charles B. Handy *The Hungry Spirit: Beyond Capitalism: A Quest for Purpose in the Modern World*. 1st edn, Broadway Books (1998).

3   'Employee Value Proposition (EVP) postpandemic should focus on the why' in Gartner. www.gartner.com/smarterwithgartner/make-way-for-a-more-human-centric-employee-value-proposition [accessed 13 June 2023].

4   'Employee Value Proposition (EVP) postpandemic should focus on the why' in Gartner. www.gartner.com/smarterwithgartner/make-way-for-a-more-human-centric-employee-value-proposition [accessed 17 March 2023].

5   'The science of predictive performance' in Contexis. www.contexis.com/ [accessed 13 June 2023].

6   Micael Johnstone. 'Brief book info.' Received by Philippa White (20 April 2023).

7   The Business Value of Design – McKinsey. www.mckinsey.com/capabilities/mckinsey-design/our-insights/the-business-value-of-design [accessed 19 June 2023].

8   Benjamin Brown, 'The Total Economic Impact™ of IBM's design thinking practice. How IBM drives client value and measurable outcomes with its design thinking framework', Forrester Consulting, p. 48 (February 2018). www.ibm.com/design/thinking/static/Enterprise-Design-Thinking-Report-8ab1e9e1622899654844a5fe1d760ed5.pdf

9   The Value of Design – Design Management Institute. www.dmi.org/page/DesignValue/The-Value-of-Design-.htm [accessed 24 April 2023].

10   Philippa White. *Ep:#69 Paul Skinner on Shifting the Stories That We Live and Work By*. https://tieleadership.com/podcast/paul-skinner-on-shifting-the-stories-that-we-live-and-work-by/

11   Philippa White. *Ep:#3 A Chat with Jon Steel Re TIE,*
      Al Gore & Ban Ki-Moon. https://tieleadership.com/
      podcast/a-chat-with-jon-steel-re-tie-al-gore-ban-ki-moon/

12   Jon Steel. Interview conducted by Philippa White (23 April 2023).

13   Corinne Post and Kris Byron 'Women on Boards and firm financial
      performance: A meta-analysis' in *Academy of Management Journal*, 58 (5/
      October), 1546–71 (2015). doi:10.5465/amj.2013.0319

14   Kris Byron and Corinne Post 'Women on Boards of Directors and
      corporate social performance: A meta-analysis: Women Directors and
      corporate social performance' in *Corporate Governance: An International
      Review*, 24 (4/July), 428–42 (2016). doi:10.1111/corg.12165

15   Kaitlin D. Wowak et al. 'The influence of female directors on product recall
      decisions' in *Manufacturing & Service Operations Management*, 23 (4/July),
      895–913 (2021). doi:10.1287/msom.2019.0841

16   'The carrot collective' in The Carrot Collective. www.thecarrotcollective.
      com [accessed 18 May 2023].

17   Philippa White. *Ep:#45 David Webster on the Power of Human Centric
      Organisational Culture Design.* https://tieleadership.com/podcast/david-
      webster-on-the-power-of-human-centric-organisational-culture-design/

18   'New citizenship project – strategy and innovation consultancy' in New
      Citizenship. www.newcitizenship.org.uk [accessed 18 May 2023].

19   Jon Alexander and Ariane Conrad *Citizens: Why the Key to Fixing
      Everything Is All of Us*. Canbury Press (2022).

20   Philippa White. *Ep:#43 Jon Alexander on Why the Private Sector Should Treat
      People as Citizens and Not Consumers.* https://tieleadership.com/podcast/
      jon-alexander-on-why-the-private-sector-should-treat-people-as-citizens-
      and-not-consumers/

21   Jon Alexander and Ariane Conrad *Citizens: Why the Key to Fixing
      Everything Is All of Us*. Canbury Press (2022).

22   R. H. Goddard 'That moon rocket proposition' in *Scientific American*, 124
      (9/February), 166 (1921). doi:10.1038/scientificamerican02261921-166

23   Rachel Meyer 'Patient safety update' in *Anesthesia News. Canadian
      Anesthesiologists' Society*, 24 (1), 7 (2009). www.cas.ca/CASAssets/
      Documents/Anesthesia-News/70_Volume24_Number1EN-March2009.
      pdf

24   Muriel Strode 'Wind-wafted flowers' in The Open Court (8/August),
      (1903). https://opensiuc.lib.siu.edu/ocj/vol1903/iss8/5

Chapter 5: How a company becomes more human

1   Simon Anholt *The Good Country Equation: How We Can Repair the World in One Generation.* 1ˢᵗ edn, BK, Berrett-Koehler Publishers (2020).

2   Sara Tate and Anna Vogt *The Rebuilders: Going from Setback to Comeback in Business and Beyond.* Kogan Page (2022).

3   Philippa White. *Ep:#51 Going from Setback to Comeback with Sara Tate.* https://tieleadership.com/podcast/ going-from-setback-to-comeback-with-sara-tate/

4   Philippa White. *Ep:#51 Going from Setback to Comeback with Sara Tate.* https://tieleadership.com/podcast/ going-from-setback-to-comeback-with-sara-tate/

5   Adam Smith *The Theory of Moral Sentiments.* A. Millar, Edinburgh: A. Kincaid & J. Bell (1761).

6   Philippa White. *Ep:#59 Sarah Cohen on the Force of Personal Connections.* https://tieleadership.com/podcast/ sarah-cohen-on-the-force-of-personal-connections/

7   Philippa White. *Ep:#76 Octopus Group's Simon Rogerson on 'Outbehaving' the Competition.* https://tieleadership.com/podcast/ octopus-groups-simon-rogerson-on-outbehaving-the-competition/

8   Paul Skinner *The Purpose Upgrade: Change Your Business to Save the World, Change the World to Save Your Business.* Robinson (2022).

9   Philippa White. *Ep:#69 Paul Skinner on Shifting the Stories That We Live and Work By.* https://tieleadership.com/podcast/ paul-skinner-on-shifting-the-stories-that-we-live-and-work-by/

10   'Larry Fink's annual 2022 letter to CEOs' in BlackRock. www.blackrock. com/corporate/investor-relations/larry-fink-ceo-letter [accessed 19 June 2023].

11   'Mark Carney on how the economy must yield to human values' in *The Economist.* www.economist.com/by-invitation/2020/04/16/mark-carney-on-how-the-economy-must-yield-to-human-values [accessed 6 July 2023].

12   Philippa White. *Ep:#34 Michael Jager on Designing Brands People Actually Love.* https://tieleadership.com/podcast/ michael-jager-on-designing-brands-people-actually-love/

13   Philippa White. *Ep:#72 Erik Fernholm on How Fulfilment Can Build a More Sustainable Future.* https://tieleadership.com/podcast/ erik-fernholm-on-how-fulfilment-can-build-a-more-sustainable-future/

14   John C. Maxwell *The 5 Levels of Leadership: Proven Steps to Maximize Your Potential.* First trade edition, Center Street (2013).

15   Philippa White. *Ep:#75 The Secret Ingredient to Law Firm Mishcon de Reya's Success.* https://tieleadership.com/podcast/the-secret-ingredient-to-law-firm-mishcon-de-reyas-success/

16   Phil Jackson and Hugh Delehanty *Eleven Rings: The Soul of Success.* Penguin Press (2014).

17   Steven Bartlett *Happy Sexy Millionaire: Unexpected Truths about Fulfilment, Love and Success.* Yellow Kite (2021).

18   Philippa White. *Ep:#67 Finding Your Laser Beam of Genius with Sarah Watson.* https://tieleadership.com/podcast/finding-your-laser-beam-of-genius-with-sarah-watson/

19   Philippa White. *Ep:#48 Jim Carroll on Discovering the Amplified Self.* https://tieleadership.com/podcast/jim-carroll-on-discovering-the-amplified-self/

20   Angeles Arrien *The Four-Fold Way: Walking the Paths of the Warrior, Teacher, Healer, and Visionary.* 1st edn, HarperSanFrancisco (1993).

Chapter 6: The gold dust hidden in the outside-in perspective

1   Oliver Wendell Holmes *The Autocrat of the Breakfast-Table: Every Man His Own Boswell.* Dover Publications (2015).

2   Philippa White. *Ep:#34 Michael Jager on Designing Brands People Actually Love.* https://tieleadership.com/podcast/michael-jager-on-designing-brands-people-actually-love/

3   Karen Coleman. Interview conducted by Philippa White (29 September 2022).

4   Philippa White. *Ep:#70 Jan Levy on Social Insights, the Digital Void and Human Connection.* https://tieleadership.com/podcast/jan-levy-on-social-insights-the-digital-void-and-human-connection/

5   Jan Levy. 'Book permissions.' Received by Philippa White (7 July 2023).

6   'The booth of truth' in Bloom. www.bloomnetwork.uk/booth-of-truth [accessed 19 June 2023].

7   Philippa White. *Ep:#44 Victoria Brooks on the Power of Truth as a Force for Change.* https://tieleadership.com/podcast/victoria-brooks-on-the-power-of-truth-as-a-force-for-change/

8   'The Foundation – the customer-led growth company' in The Foundation
    – The Customer-Led Growth Company. www.the-foundation.com
    [accessed 19 June 2023].

9   Charlie Dawson and Seán Meehan *The Customer Copernicus: How to Be
    Customer-led*. Routledge (2021).

10 Philippa White. *Ep:#18 Charlie Dawson on Purpose and
    Customer-Led Success*. https://tieleadership.com/podcast/
    charlie-dawson-on-purpose-and-customer-led-success/

11 Philippa White. *Ep:#75 The Secret Ingredient to Law Firm
    Mishcon de Reya's Success*. https://tieleadership.com/podcast/
    the-secret-ingredient-to-law-firm-mishcon-de-reyas-success/

Chapter 7: The human stories behind corporate successes

1   Equity and Diversity, University of Gloucestershire [online] (12 December
    2018). https://sites.glos.ac.uk/equity/2018/12/12/without-continual-
    growth-and-progress-such-words-as-improvement-achievement-and-
    success-have-no-meaning-benjamin-franklin/

2   Comunidade dos Pequenos Profetas – Uma organização
    não-governamental, sem fins lucrativos (4 September 2020). http://
    pequenosprofetas.org.br/

3   White Pencil Winner – Recipeace. www.youtube.com/
    watch?v=ZNQfNZK2DQA [accessed 15 May 2023].

4   Philippa White. *Ep:#76 Octopus Group's Simon Rogerson on
    'Outbehaving' the Competition*. https://tieleadership.com/podcast/
    octopus-groups-simon-rogerson-on-outbehaving-the-competition/

5   'GOOD Agency – purpose driven strategy and creative agency' in GOOD
    Agency. www.goodagency.co.uk/ [accessed 15 May 2023].

6   Philippa White. *Ep:#77 Chris Norman from GOOD on Making a Difference
    by Changing the System*. https://tieleadership.com/podcast/chris-norman-
    from-good-on-making-a-difference-by-changing-the-system/

7   Philippa White. *Ep:#77 Chris Norman from GOOD on Making a Difference
    by Changing the System*. https://tieleadership.com/podcast/chris-norman-
    from-good-on-making-a-difference-by-changing-the-system/

8   B Lab Global Site. www.bcorporation.net/en-us [accessed 27 April 2023].

9   'Lactation pods for work + public spaces' in Mamava. www.mamava.com
    [accessed 24 March 2023].

10   Philippa White. *Ep:#47 Sascha Mayer on How Disruptive Design Can Impact Lives*. https://tieleadership.com/podcast/sascha-mayer-on-how-disruptive-design-can-impact-lives/

11   'Medela and Mamava join forces to support working families and employers' in Medela. www.medela.us/breastfeeding/media-center/medela-and-mamava-join-forces-to-support-working-families-and-employers [accessed 24 March 2023].

12   Philippa White. *Ep:#49 The Future Direction of Patagonia with Whitney Clapper*. https://tieleadership.com/podcast/the-future-direction-of-patagonia-with-whitney-clapper/

13   Jane Denton 'Top 10 UK companies for customer service revealed' in This Is Money (26 January 2023). www.thisismoney.co.uk/money/markets/article-11679259/Top-10-UK-companies-customer-service-revealed.html

14   John Sills *The Human Experience: How to Make Life Better for Your Customers and Create a More Successful Organization*. Bloomsbury Business (2023).

15   Philippa White. *Ep:#71 John Sills on the Human Experience*. https://tieleadership.com/podcast/john-sills-on-the-human-experience/

16   Man from the Pru. www.prudentialplc.com/en/about-us/our-history/man-from-the-pru [accessed 26 June 2023].

17   Philippa White. *Ep:#64 Human Emotion and Architecture with Heatherwick's Eliot Postma*. https://tieleadership.com/podcast/human-emotion-and-architecture-with-heatherwicks-eliot-postma/

18   'Heatherwick Studio – Design & Architecture' in Heatherwick Studio – Design & Architecture. www.heatherwick.com/ [accessed 16 June 2023].

19   'Heatherwick Studio – Design & Architecture – Maggie's Yorkshire' in Heatherwick Studio – Design & Architecture. www.heatherwick.com/project/maggies/ [accessed 16 June 2023].

20   'Heatherwick Studio – Design & Architecture – New Routemaster' in Heatherwick Studio – Design & Architecture. www.heatherwick.com/project/new-routemaster/ [accessed 16 June 2023].

21   'Heatherwick Studio – Design & Architecture – Google Bay View' in Heatherwick Studio – Design & Architecture. www.heatherwick.com/projects/buildings/google-bay-view/ [accessed 16 June 2023].

22   Heatherwick Studio – LinkedIn. www.linkedin.com/posts/heatherwick-studio_buildingtocop27-activity-6997119887525445632-SY_E/?utm_source=share&utm_medium=member_desktop [accessed 16 June 2023].

23   Google Bay View – BIG + Heatherwick Studio' in ArchDaily (14 July 2022). www.archdaily.com/985328/google-bay-view-big-plus-heatherwick-studio

Chapter 8: Creating the necessary conditions for magic to happen

1   *Best of Bullmore.* www.bestofbullmore.com/about [accessed 19 June 2023].

2   Jeremy Bullmore *The Quality Quotient: or How I Made the World a Better Place.* Writersworld (2017).

3   'Your questions answered: What is Bhutan's Gross National Happiness Index?' in Asian Development Blog. https://blogs.adb.org/blog/your-questions-answered-what-bhutan-s-gross-national-happiness-index#:~:text=The%20Gross%20National%20Happiness%20(GNH,organized%20by%20the%20United%20Nations [accessed 18 June 2023].

4   'Gross National Happiness (GNH): Definition of index and 4 pillars' in Investopedia. www.investopedia.com/terms/g/gnh.asp [accessed 19 June 2023].

5   Elizabeth Piper and Michael Holden, 'Britain's "freedom Day" will come on July 19, says Government' in *Reuters* (28 June 2021). www.reuters.com/business/retail-consumer/uk-looks-set-ease-restrictions-july-19-sun-cites-pm-saying-2021-06-28/

6   Philippa White. *Ep:#65 Prison Radio and It's Power with Phil Maguire.* https://tieleadership.com/podcast/prison-radio-and-its-power-with-phil-maguire/

7   Prison Radio (12 February 2021). www.prisonradio.org/

8   Philippa White. *Ep:#69 Paul Skinner on Shifting the Stories That We Live and Work By.* https://tieleadership.com/podcast/paul-skinner-on-shifting-the-stories-that-we-live-and-work-by/

9   Paul Skinner *Collaborative Advantage: How Collaboration Beats Competition as a Strategy for Success.* Robinson, an imprint of Little, Brown Book Group (2018).

Chapter 9: The world is a global village, and we are all responsible for its future

1   David Mitchell *Cloud Atlas.* 1st US edn, Random House Trade Paperbacks (2004).

2   Max Roser and Hannah Ritchie, 'HIV / AIDS' in Our World in Data (April 2018). https://ourworldindata.org/hiv-aids

3   Cameron Bowie, 'The burden of disease in Malawi' in *Malawi Medical Journal: The Journal of Medical Association of Malawi*, 18 (3/September), 103–10 (2006). www.ncbi.nlm.nih.gov/pmc/articles/PMC3345623/

4   'Home – Sustainable Cleaner Cooking Coalition' in Cleaner Cooking.
     www.cleanercooking.org [accessed 30 September 2023].

5   'Spicing up the cooking challenge: 2.8 billion or 4 billion?' in World
     Bank Blogs (21 January 2021). https://blogs.worldbank.org/energy/
     spicing-cooking-challenge-28-billion-or-4-billion

6   Mikel González-Eguino, 'Energy poverty: An overview' in *Renewable
     and Sustainable Energy Reviews*, 47, 377–85 (July 2015). doi:10.1016/j.
     rser.2015.03.013

7   'CCA, AGF, and UNCDF launch partnership to mobilize $100 million
     for clean cooking' in Clean Cooking Alliance. https://cleancooking.org/
     news/cca-agf-and-uncdf-launch-partnership-to-mobilize-100-million-
     for-clean-cooking/ [accessed 26 September 2023].

8   'CCA, AGF, and UNCDF launch partnership to mobilize $100 million
     for clean cooking' in Clean Cooking Alliance. https://cleancooking.org/
     news/cca-agf-and-uncdf-launch-partnership-to-mobilize-100-million-
     for-clean-cooking/ [accessed 26 September 2023].

9   'Sustainable Development Goals – United Nations Development
     Programme' in UNDP. www.undp.org/sustainable-development-goals/
     affordable-and-clean-energy [accessed 26 June 2023].

10   Philippa White. *Ep:#32 Luca Zerbini on unearthing the solution to an
     unknown climate challenge.* https://tieleadership.com/podcast/luca-zerbini-
     on-unearthing-the-solution-to-an-unknown-climate-challenge/

11   Leonard Cohen *Anthem.* Columbia (24 November 1992). https://open.
     spotify.com/track/7aAE5KL20Uycf3dswsaHjp?si=cbabc42bbd66420f

12   Peter Certo 'Brazil's World Cup evictions: An insult to soccer – FPIF'
     in Foreign Policy In Focus (10 February 2014). https://fpif.org/
     brazils-world-cup-evictions-insult-soccer/

13   *Habitat for Humanity.* www.habitat.org/ [accessed 21 June 2023].

14   'Brazil 2014 showed once again why sponsors need to grow some
     balls' in Campaign. www.campaignlive.co.uk/article/brazil-2014-
     showed-once-again-why-sponsors-need-grow-balls/1307051?utm_
     source=website&utm_medium=social [accessed 6 July 2023].

15   'Brazil 2014 showed once again why sponsors need to grow some
     balls' in Campaign. www.campaignlive.co.uk/article/brazil-2014-
     showed-once-again-why-sponsors-need-grow-balls/1307051?utm_
     source=website&utm_medium=social [accessed 6 July 2023].

16   'FIFA sets up Human Rights Panel in response to criticism'
     in Reuters (10 March 2017). www.reuters.com/article/
     us-soccer-fifa-rights-idUSKBN16H1LC

17   'Malawi: Children working on tobacco farms remain out of school, say UN Experts' in OHCHR. www.ohchr.org/en/press-releases/2022/12/malawi-children-working-tobacco-farms-remain-out-school-say-un-experts [accessed 6 July 2023].

18   Joel Goldberg 'It takes a village to determine the origins of an African proverb' in *NPR* (30 July 2016). www.npr.org/sections/goatsandsoda/2016/07/30/487925796/it-takes-a-village-to-determine-the-origins-of-an-african-proverb

19   'Future first Kenya' in Alumni Kenya. https://alumnikenya.org/about-us/ [accessed 21 June 2023].

20   'Future first Kenya' in Alumni Kenya. https://alumnikenya.org/about-us/ [accessed 21 June 2023].

Chapter 10: The opportunities out there waiting to be embraced

1   Philippa White. *Ep:#48 Jim Carroll on Discovering the Amplified Self.* https://tieleadership.com/podcast/jim-carroll-on-discovering-the-amplified-self/

2   Tomas Björkman 'How to use personal, inner development to build strong democracies' 1534784130. https://www.ted.com/talks/tomas_bjorkman_the_nordic_secret_how_to_use_personal_inner_development_to_build_strong_democracies

3   Tomas Björkman 'The Nordic Secret: How to use inner development to build strong democracies' www.youtube.com/watch?v=7dswOT3rAKc [accessed 21 June 2023].

4   'Inner development goals' in Inner Development Goals. www.innerdevelopmentgoals.org [accessed 23 June 2023].

5   Philippa White. *Ep:#72 Erik Fernholm on How Fulfilment Can Build a More Sustainable Future.* https://tieleadership.com/podcast/erik-fernholm-on-how-fulfilment-can-build-a-more-sustainable-future/

6   Our History – Highlander Research and Education Center. https://highlandercenter.org/our-history-timeline/ [accessed 23 June 2023].

7   'Highlander folk school and the criminalization of organizing' in The Rebellious Life of Mrs. Rosa Parks (16 May 2016). https://rosaparksbiography.org/bio/highlander-folk-school-and-the-criminalization-of-organizing/

8   Sarah Polus, 'Full transcript of President Obama's toast at the Nordic State Dinner' in *The Washington Post* (13 May 2016). www.

washingtonpost.com/news/reliable-source/wp/2016/05/13/
full-transcript-of-president-obamas-toast-at-the-nordic-state-dinner/

9   Stockholm,Visionary Films. Inner Development Goals film. EngSubs.
    2021. https://vimeo.com/657361309

10 Miguel de Unamuno *Essays and Soliloquies*. Knopf (1924).

11 'Iracambi: Saving forests and changing lives in the Brazilian rainforest' in
    Iracambi. https://iracambi.com/ [accessed 7 June 2023].

12 Philippa White. *Ep:#69 Paul Skinner on Shifting the Stories
    That We Live and Work By*. https://tieleadership.com/podcast/
    paul-skinner-on-shifting-the-stories-that-we-live-and-work-by/

13 Gib Bulloch *The Intrapreneur: Confessions of a Corporate Insurgent*. Unbound
    (2018).

14 Gib Bulloch, 'Be the change you want to see in your company' in
    TEDxPlainpalais. www.youtube.com/watch?v=5KYWJdU9Ltw [accessed
    21 June 2023].

15 Gib Bulloch *The Intrapreneur: Confessions of a Corporate Insurgent*. Unbound
    (2018).

16 Philippa White. *Ep:#66 How to Stop Men Taking Their Own
    Lives with Ben Akers*. https://tieleadership.com/podcast/
    how-to-stop-men-taking-their-own-lives-with-ben-akers/

17 How Zume Became a Packaging Innovator. www.linkedin.com/pulse/
    how-zume-become-packaging-innovator-alex-garden [accessed 6 July
    2023].

18 Philippa White. *Ep:#27 Alex Garden and the Solution to
    a Plastic Free World*. https://tieleadership.com/podcast/
    alex-garden-and-the-solution-to-a-plastic-free-world/

19 'Brand Naming – Brand Packaging – Brand Naming – Product
    Development' in BOLTGROUP. https://boltgroup.com/work/gigs2go/
    [accessed 11 July 2023].

20 'Kaffeeform – Cups from recycled coffee grounds' in Kaffeeform. www.
    kaffeeform.com/en/ [accessed 26 June 2023].

21 Rollo May *Man's Search for Himself*. Norton (2009).

22 Philippa White. *Ep:#72 Erik Fernholm on How Fulfilment Can
    Build a More Sustainable Future*. https://tieleadership.com/podcast/
    erik-fernholm-on-how-fulfilment-can-build-a-more-sustainable-future/

Index

29k Foundation 123

academic learning 27
accountability 114–117
Accra, Ghana: Golden Baobab Prize 40
Achievers 67
action 126–127
adaptability 6–7
adversity 21
African Bureau Stories 41
African literacy 40–41
African National Congress (ANC) xvii,
    xviii, 36
agency 31–33
Agency of the Year 2023 80
Ahenkorah, Deborah 40–41
Airbnb 59
Akers, Ben: Talk Club 129–130
Alexander, Jon 52–53
Allan, Chloe 116–117
alumni 118
Amos, Gerald xvi
Analysts 67
Anholt, Simon: *The Good Country Equation*
    58
Archetype 72
architecture 91
Arendt, Hannah 45
Arrien, Dr Angeles: *The Four Fold Way* 67
authenticity 88
Ave Rara 68–69

Baker, Ella 123
balance 53–54, 103

Bartle Bogle Hegarty (BBH) 19
Bartlett, Steven 65
'beginner's mind' 30
belonging 10–11
Bhutan: Gross National Happiness (GNH)
    99
Björkman, Tomas 122
Bloom UK 73–74
Bolsonaro 13
Bolsonaro, Jair 57, 58
Booth of Truth, The 73–74
Bovarnick, Andrew 124
Bowie, David 29, 30
brands 62–63
Brazil 15, 57–58
    2014 FIFA World Cup 111–113
    Affective Kitchens 32
    Atlantic Forest 15
    caprichar 25–26
    Comitè Popular da Copa 111
    COVID-19 pandemic 31–34
    favelas 111
    human rights 111
    Iracambi 15, 125
    Nos Valemos Mais 112
    Olympics 111
    perseverence with passion 22–24
    Recife 81, 112
breast pumps 86
breastfeeding 86
bringing out the best in leaders 79–92
Bristol Beer Factory: Clear Head 130
British Red Cross 83
Brooks, Victoria 73

Brown, Brené 10
Brunwin, Siobhan 74
Bullmore, Jeremy 97–98, 103
  The Quality Quotient 98
Bulloch, Gib: *The Intrapreneur: Confessions
    of a Corporate Insurgent* 128
Burnett, Leo 79, 81
Burton Snowboards 71
Business of Creativity, The 19
business paradigms 45
  business as usual failing to benefit all
      53–55
  in business to save the home planet
      86–88
  companies at the service of their people
      51–52
  hiring good humans, not just leaders
      49–51
  main goal of business 45–49

c 22
C4C (Chance for Change) 115
Canada 3
  Manitoba 3–4
  Ontario 4, 5
  University of Winnipeg 4–5
Canadian Anesthesiologists' Society (CAS)
      54
caprichar 25–26
Carpenter, Jake 71–72
Carroll, Jim 66, 121–122
Carrot Collective, The 52
CCC (The Cleaner Cooking Coalition)
      107–109
certainty 9–10
Chaco footwear 87
challenges 20–21
Chance for Change (C4C) 115–11, 116
  Entrepreneurship Programme 115
charity sector 83
children's literature 40
Circular Economy 130–131
Citizens 52
Clapper, Whitney 86–88
climate change xx, 137n6
climate crisis 87–88
Cohen, Leonard 110
Cohen, Sarah 59
cohesion 15
Coleman, Karen 72

collaboration 11–12, 15, 100
comfort zones 17–19
Communidade dos Pequenos Profetas
      (CPP) 81
companies xxi
compassion 31–33
connection with others 3–5, 10–11
Conrad, Ariane 53
constraints 20–22
Consumer Story 52–53
Contexis 47–48
conversations 58
coral reefs 14–15
Corney, Mark 62
corporate successes *see* human stories
      behind corporate successes
courage 10
COVID-19 pandemic 31–34, 101
CPP (Communidade dos Pequenos
      Profetas) 81
CQ (cultural intelligence) 11–13, 20
creating connections 3–5
creating more human leaders and
      companies 43
  gold dust hidden in outside-in
      perspective 71–77
  how a company becomes more human
      57–69
  human stories behind corporate
      successes 79–93
  problem with old business paradigms
      45–55
creating necessary conditions for magic 97
  power of building mutually beneficial
      relationships 103–104
  power of forging unlikely partnerships
      99–101
  power of integrating humanity into
      financial equation 97–99
  power of reintegrating people into
      society 101–103
cultural intelligence (CQ) 11–12, 15, 20
curiosity 13, 19, 20, 22, 63, 75, 90, 131
*Customer Copernicus: How to be Customer-
      led, The* 74–75

D&AD White Pencil 81
Dalai Lama xvi, 26
Dawson, Charlie 74–75
deforestation 15

dependence on others 14–16
determination 39
Diana, Princess 65
Dijalma 33
doubt 9
dreams 127
Dyer, Wayne 24

education 27–28, 82
egos 7–9
Ekskäret Foundatiion 123
Electric Radio Brixton 102
'Elephant, Dead fish and Vomit' 59
emotional intelligence (EQ) 12
empathy 33–34
employee owned businesses 85
empowerment 88
Epictetus 26
Exchange, The 74
experiential learning 27–29, 75, 82
expertise 9–10
experts 30

Facebook 112
fantasy 127
Fernando de Noronha 68
Fernholm, Erik 63, 123, 126, 132
FIFA World Cup 112, 113–114
final challenge 127–131
finding your humanity 1
    impact of using human assets 31–41
    special human ingredients 3–16
    what liberates our human assets? 17–30
Fink, Larry 62
first direct 89
flexibility 6–7
foreword xv–xvi
Foundation, The 89
Franklin, Benjamin 79
Freire, Paulo 27
fuel stacking 108
'full-hearted' people 10
Future First Kenya 118–119

Garage Soho, The 19
Garden, Alex 130
Gebbia, Jo 59
gender equality 73
Ghana 40
Gigs 2 Go 130

Gilley, Trevor 106–107, 110
Global North 100
global perspective 14
Global South 7, 100
Goddard, Robert H. 53
gold dust hidden in outside-in perspective
    71
    real people in the driver's seat 71–76
    treating the planet as customer 76–77
GOOD 83–84, 85
Google: Bay View Campus 92
Greenpeace 83
grit 24, 30, 39
Guardian newspaper 97
Guga 23, 28, 68–69

Habitat for Humanity 111
Heatherwick Studio 91–92
Heggarty, Sir John 19–20
Holmes, Oliver Wendell Sr 71
honesty 88
Honnold, Alex 18
Hooper, Alice 80–81
'human,' defined xx–xxi
human assets xxi, 3, 129
    checking egos at the door 7–9
    connection and belonging 10–11
    creating connections 3–5
    cultural intelligence and collaboration
        11–12, 20
    dependence on others 14–16
    flexibility and adaptability 6–7
    my way or the highway 9–10
    ripple effect 12–13
    see also liberating our human assets:
        powers
human assets: impact of using 31, 34–36
    compassion and agency 31–33
    empathy 33–34
    expanding perspectives 39–41
    inner compass 36–38
    resilience 38–39
    self-awareness xx–xxi, 34–36, 100
human rights
    Jiyan Foundation for Human Rights
        15–16, 35
    and the World Cup 111, 112, 113–114
human stories behind corporate successes
    79
    bringing out the best in leaders 79–82

in business to save the home planet
86–88
long-lasting relationships over short-
term efficiency 89–91
purpose-driven business: from humans to
humans 83–86
humanity
in the financial equation 97–99
at the heart of design 47, 88, 91–93
leadership training 129
purpose-driven business 83–86
humility 3
hurricanes 14

Ian White Patient Safety Award 54
iClima Earth 109
Ideas Unlimited 83
IDGs *see* Inner Development Goals
impact of using human assets 31
compassion and agency 31–33
empathy 33–34
expanding perspectives 39–41
following your inner compass 36–38
resilience 38–39
self-awareness/living a life with intention
34–36
individuals xxi
inner compass 36–38
Inner Development Goals (IDGs) 63,
123–124, 126
innovation 20
Institute of Customer Service 89
intelligence quotient (IQ) 12
interconnectedness xxi, 14, 100
interdependence xxi, 14, 100
intermediate technology 108
intrapreneurs 47, 128
introduction: a leader driven by his
humanity xvii–xxii
invitation 131–132
IQ (intelligence quotient) 12
Iraq
ISIS invasion of Sinjar 35
Jiyan Foundation for Human Rights
15–16, 35
IsiXhosa xviii, 137n4

J. Walter Thompson 97
Jackson, Phil 65
Jacobson, Rae 6

Jager, Michael 22, 62, 71, 86
Jiyan Foundation for Human Rights
15–16, 35
Jodorowsky, Alejandro xvi, 22
Johnstone, Micael 47
José de Goya y Lucientes, Francisco 121

Kaffeeform 130
Karve, Dr Priyadarshini 108
Kenya: education 117–118
kindness 3, 68, 85
Kota, Zo xviii
Kurdistan 15, 35–36

lactation suites 86
leadership xvii–xxii, 51, 64–65, 79–82,
128, 129
learning 27–29
LEED Platinum buildings 92
LEGO Group 51
Leo Burnett Change Chicago 81
Leo Burnett London 80, 82
lessons from a hummingbird 124–127
Levy, Jan 72–73, 90
liberating our human assets: powers 17
of a beginner's mind 29–30
constraints 20–22
disrupting zones of comfort 17–19
of lived experience 27–29
perseverance with passion 22–24
positive mindset 24–27
wonder 19–20
Ligoya, Dr Perks 109
literacy 40
lived experience 27–29
local problems are not isolated issues
105–110
long-lasting relationships over short-term
efficiency 89–91
Lula da Silva, Luiz Inácio 57, 58

Macmillan Cancer Support 83
Maguire, Phil 102
Malawi 7, 105–109, 114–117
CCC (The Cleaner Cooking Coalition)
107
Chance for Change (C4C) 115–116
cooking 105–108
Criminal Justice system 115
education 114–115

HIV and Aids 115
UN HIgh-Level Dialogue on Energy
     108
  wood 105–106
Mamava 85
management 51
Mandela, Nelson xvii, xviii, 36
Marine Megafauna Foundation (MMF) 76
Mars 83–84
Maser, Omar 106–107
'maternal wall' 52
Maxwell, John C. 64
May, Rollo 131
Mayer, Sascha 86
meaning 85
Medela 86
mental capacity 73
Merrell 87
Meso American Reef Fund (MAR Fund)
     14
M&G plc 90–91
Michelangelo 13
micro-gasification 108
Middleton, Judith 12
Miguel de Unamuno 124
Miller, Gina: Article 50 65
Mishcon de Reya 65
Mitchell, David 105
MMF (Marine Megafauna Foundation) 76
more human-centred companies 57
  celebrating egoless leadership and shared
       purpose 68–69
  creating a happy working climate 63–64
  creating space to empower others 64–65
  fostering relationships 57–61
  having a north star that resonates with
       people 61–63
  trusting the strength of difference 65–68
Moss, Elliot 65, 75
Mozambique 76
mutually beneficial relationships 103–104
my way or the highway 9–10
#MyFuture Pledge 119

National Medical and Dental Association
     (NAMDA) xvii–xviii, 137n2
National Prison Radio (NPR) 102–103
negative emotions 26
Nepal
  Chance for Change (C4C) 115

neuroscience 123
NeverEnding Story, The 127
New Citizenship Project 52
New Division, The 123
Newick, Dick 68
Next15 117, 118
Nin, Anaïs 7, 110, 138n4
Nordic Secret 122–123
Norman, Chris 83–85
NPR (National Prison Radio) 102–103
Nurturers 67

Obama, Barack 123
Octopus Group 60, 82, 116
Ojai (Unceded Territory of the CHumash,
     Southern California) 87
Okoth, Ken 118
old business paradigms 45–55
Olins, Rufus 98
Olsen, Erik 6n2, 138n2
opportunities waiting to be embraced 121
  an invitation 131–132
  a final challenge 127–131
  lessons from a hummingbird 124–127
  ripples of possibility 121–124
outcome of the return on humanity 95
  creating necessary conditions for magic
       97–104
  opportunities waiting to be embraced
       121–122
  the world is a global village 105–120
outside-in perspective 71, 100
  the planet as another customer 76–77
  real people in the driver's seat 71–76
owntruths 74

Packard, David 46
Parks, Rosa 123
passion 22–24
Patagonia xv–xvi
  Community Engagement + Impact
       86–88
  footwear 87
people's power 100
perfection 10
performance appraisals 66
permaculture 103
perseverance with passion 22–24
perspectives 39–41
Phike, Lizzie xviii–xix

plastic packaging 130
positive mindset 24–27
Postma, Eliot 91–92
Powell, Sir Chris 97
powers *see* liberating our human assets: powers
Prison Radio Association (PRA) 102
private sector: leveraging the power 110–114
Prudential 90
psychological safety 58
Publicis.Poke 80
purpose 85
purpose-driven business: from humans to humans 83–86

Recife, Brazil 81
Red Bus, London 92
Refeno Regatta, Brazil 68
reflection 9–10
reintegration into society 101–103
relationships 57–60, 89–91
resilience 6–7, 21, 22, 27, 28, 38–39
resourcefulness 21
responsibility xvi
return on humanity 99, 110
ripple effect 13–16
ripples of possibility 121–124
Rogerson, Simon 60, 82
Roosevelt, Eleanor 21
Rosling, John 48
Roth, Christa 108
Rudd, Charlie 80

Salih, Asmaa Ibrahim M. 15–16, 35
saving the planet 86–88
Scandinavia: folk high schools 122
schools 82, 122
SDGs *see* Sustainable Development Goals
self-awareness xx–xxi, 16, 28, 34–36, 100
self-interest 103
shrinking divides to make the world more human 117–120
Sills, John: *The Human Experience* 89–90
Sirolli, Ernesto 8–9
Skinner, Paul 48, 127
    Collaborative Advantage 103
    The Purpose Upgrade 61–62
Smith, Adam: *The Invisible Hand* 59
Smith, Arthur 40

Smith, Lauren 76–77
Solidarity of Unbridled Labour 22, 62, 71, 86
Sorrell, Sir Martin 51
South Africa xvii–xix
    African National Congress (ANC) xvii, xviii, 34–36
    Chamber of Mines 36
    gold mining 36–37
    Natives Land Act (1913) 36
special human ingredients 3, 15, 100
    checking egos at the door 7–9
    connection and belonging 10–11
    creating connections 3–5
    cultural intelligence and collaboration 11–12, 15, 20, 100
    flexibility and adaptability 6–7
    my way or the highway 9–10
    the ripple effect and our dependence on others 13–16
Steel, Jon 49–50, 71, 97–98, 111
Strode, Muriel 55
Sturgeon, Nicola 109
success 125–126
Sustainable Development Goals (SDGs) 108, 123
Swedish Armed Forces 63
Syria 15–16
Systems7 28

Talk Club 129–130
Tanzania 38
    Songambele 39
Tate, Sara and Anna Vogt: *The Rebuilders* 21, 58–59
Tembo, Hon Nancy 109
Thailand 11–12, 13–14, 104
Theobald, Sam 117
theoretical learning 27
Three Hands 72–73, 90
TIE xvi, 19, 80, 81, 98, 108–109, 118
Tolipova-Gourdin, Gulshanoy 51

Una Terra 109
Unceded Territory of the Chumash, Southern California (Ojai) 87
UNESCO 40
United Democratic Front (UDF) xviii, 137n3
United Nations 123

High-Level Dialogue on Energy 108
SDG7 (Sustainable Development Goal
    7) 108
unlikely partnerships 99–101
Urassa, Faustina 38–39

value 62
vision and Visionaries 67, 85
Vogt, Anna *see* Tate, Sara and Anna Vogt
Voltaire 9
vulnerability 3, 9–10

wabi sabi 25
Walker, Sarah 111–112, 113–114
Watson, Sarah 66
Webster, David 52
Wheatley, Rick 28
White, Ian 53–54
White, Neil xvii–xix, 37–38, 137n1
Wieden and Kennedy New York 106
wonder 19–20
world, the xxi

World Cup 111, 112, 113–114
world is a global village 105
    bringing out the best through
        accountability 114–117
    leveraging the power of the private
        sector 110–114
    local problems are not isolated issues
        105–110
    shrinking divides to make the world
        more human 117–120
WPP 97
WPP Fellowship 49–51, 71, 111

Y2K bug 13
Yeung, Johnny xv

Zambia 8–9
Zen Buddhism 30
Zerbini, Luca 109–110
Ziglar, Zig 81
zones of comfort 17–19

A quick word from Practical Inspiration Publishing...

We hope you found this book both practical and inspiring – that's what we aim for with every book we publish.

We publish titles on topics ranging from leadership, entrepreneurship, HR and marketing to self-development and wellbeing.

Find details of all our books at: www.practicalinspiration.com

 **Did you know...**

We can offer discounts on bulk sales of all our titles – ideal if you want to use them for training purposes, corporate giveaways or simply because you feel these ideas deserve to be shared with your network.

We can even produce bespoke versions of our books, for example with your organization's logo and/or a tailored foreword.

To discuss further, contact us on info@practicalinspiration.com.

 Got an idea for a business book?

We may be able to help. Find out more about publishing in partnership with us at: bit.ly/PIpublishing.

Follow us on social media...